# HREE SQUARES

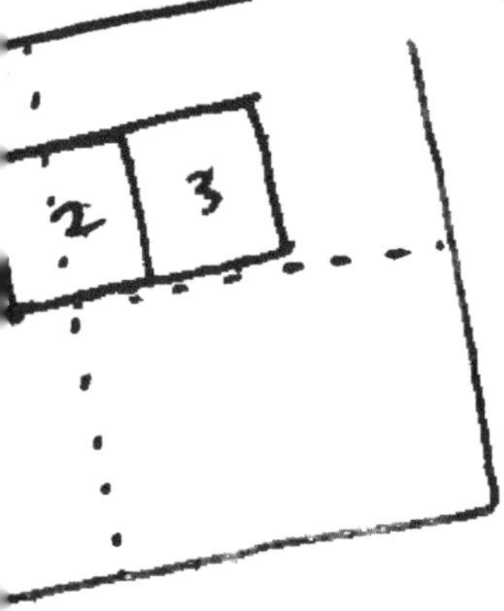

## TRIANGLE BELOW

E, SQUARE #3

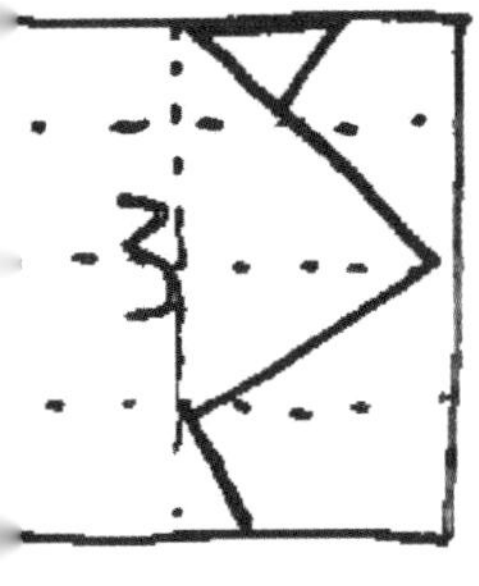

④ WESTSI

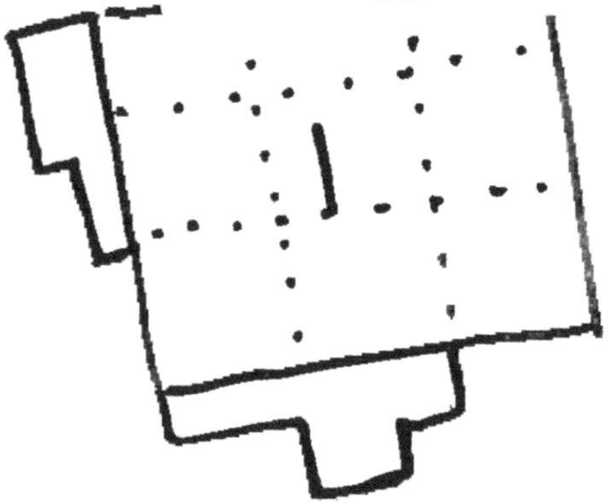

⑤ SOUTHWEST, TRIANGLE

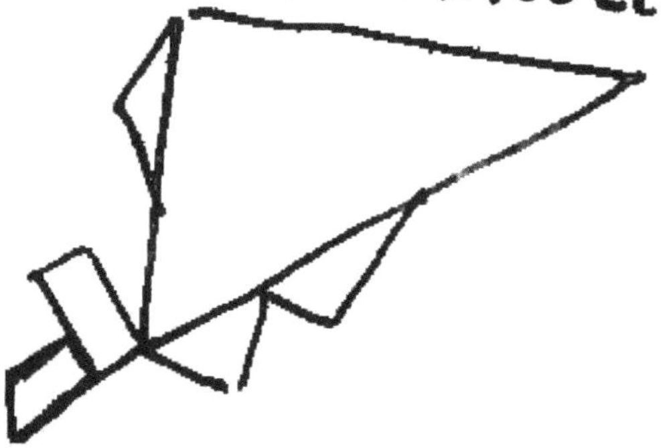

⑥ TRACE HAND TO ADD SPOKE STREETS

# Detroit in 50 Maps

MAP OF THE
CENTRAL BUSINESS DISTRICT
of
DETROIT 1904
MICHIGAN
Sanborn Map Company
11 BROADWAY, NEW YORK

Scale 200 Feet to an inch

DETROIT

KEY
Fire proof construction
Brick building
Frame
Equipped with automatic sprinklers
Fire engine house
Steam R.R. Tracks

# Detroit in 50 Maps

Alex B. Hill

**Belt Publishing**
**Cleveland, OH**

Printed in the United States of America
First edition 2021
ISBN: 978-1-953368-02-7

Belt Publishing
5322 Fleet Avenue
Cleveland, Ohio 44105
www.beltpublishing.com

"There are cities that get by on their good looks.
Detroit has to work for a living."
**—ELMORE LEONARD**

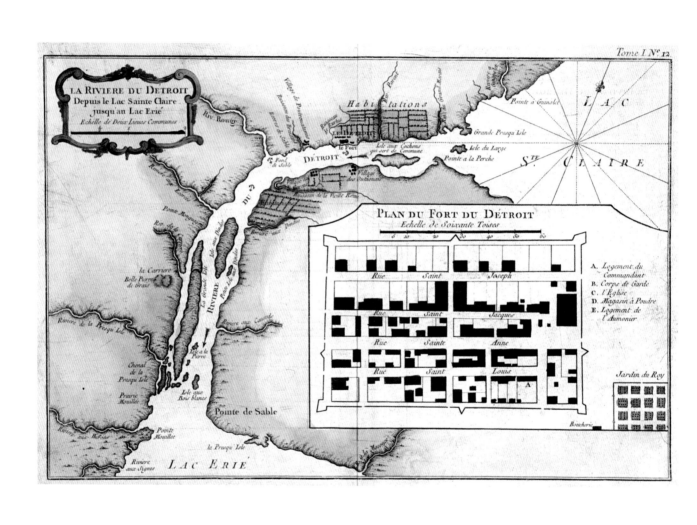

LA RIVIERE DU DÉTROIT
Depuis le Lac Sainte Claire
jusqu'au Lac Erié
Echelle de Deux Lieues Communes

PLAN DU FORT DU DÉTROIT
Echelle de Soixante Toises

Riie     Saint     Joseph
Rue     Saint     Jacques
Rue     Sainte     Anne
Rue     Saint     Louis

A. Logement du Commandant
B. Corps de Garde
C. l'Eglise
D. Magasin à Poudre
E. Logement de l'Aumonier

Jardin du Roy

Boucherie

LAC STE CLAIRE

Pointe à Gunolet
Grande Presqu Isle
Isle du Large
Pointe a la Perche

HABITATIONS
Village de Pontouatamis
LE FORT du DÉTROIT
Isle aux Cochons qui sert de Commune
le Fort
DÉTROIT
Village des Outnouais
Riv. Rouge
Fond de Sable
Ruisseau de la Vieille Reine
Village

RIVIERE DU DÉTROIT
Les Grande Isle
Petite Isle aux Dindes
Isle aux Dindes
Riviere aux Dindes

Rentée aux Loutres
Pointe Montagny
Riv. aux Dindes
la Carriere
Belle Pierre de Grais
Riviere de la Presqu Isle
Chenal de la Presqu Isle
Prairie Mouillée
Isle à la Perre
Isle aux Bois blancs
Pointe de Sable
Pointe Mouillée
Riviere aux Mafzes
la Presqu Isle
Riviere aux Cignes

LAC ERIÉ

We map these lands, but they are not ours.

The author and publisher of this book acknowledge the history of Waawiyatanong (what is now called Detroit, Michigan) and wish to honor the indigenous people who continue to steward this land.

# TABLE OF CONTENTS

**Author's Note** 11 | **Editor's Note** 13 | **Introduction** 15

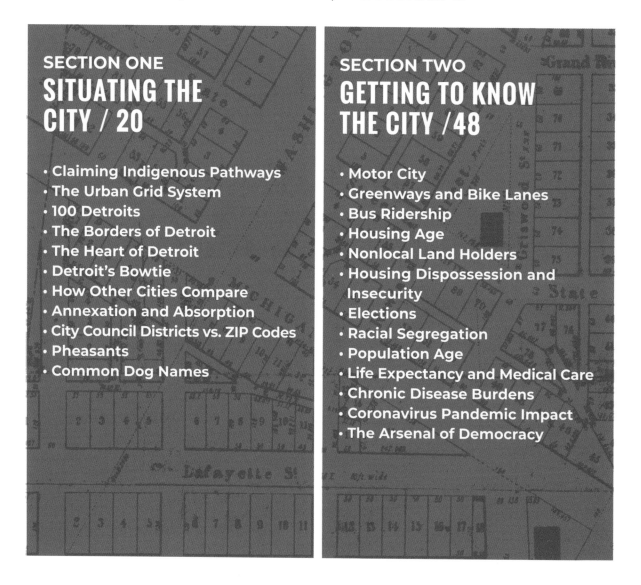

## SECTION ONE
## SITUATING THE CITY / 20

- Claiming Indigenous Pathways
- The Urban Grid System
- 100 Detroits
- The Borders of Detroit
- The Heart of Detroit
- Detroit's Bowtie
- How Other Cities Compare
- Annexation and Absorption
- City Council Districts vs. ZIP Codes
- Pheasants
- Common Dog Names

## SECTION TWO
## GETTING TO KNOW THE CITY /48

- Motor City
- Greenways and Bike Lanes
- Bus Ridership
- Housing Age
- Nonlocal Land Holders
- Housing Dispossession and Insecurity
- Elections
- Racial Segregation
- Population Age
- Life Expectancy and Medical Care
- Chronic Disease Burdens
- Coronavirus Pandemic Impact
- The Arsenal of Democracy

**Sources** 137 | **About the Author** 141

SECTION THREE
# COMMUNITIES AND NEIGHBORHOODS / 78

- (Dis)Agreement Lines
- First Neighborhood Names of Detroit
- Changes in the Land: Corktown & Hamtramck
- The Legacy of Redlining
- The Green Book
- Governance and Neighborhood Areas
- Investment Zones
- Midtown Creation and Expansion
- Cass Corridor vs. Midtown
- Eastern Market Regional Foodshed
- Eastern Market Murals vs. Graffiti
- Heidelberg Art Artifacts

SECTION FOUR
# PLACES IN THE CITY / 110

- Colleges and Universities
- Coffee Shops
- Coworking Spaces
- Grocery Stores
- Fast Food
- Coney Dogs
- Park Spaces
- Community Gardens
- Churches and Liquor Stores
- Pharmacies
- Civic Technology and Business Incubators
- Detroit Hand Map

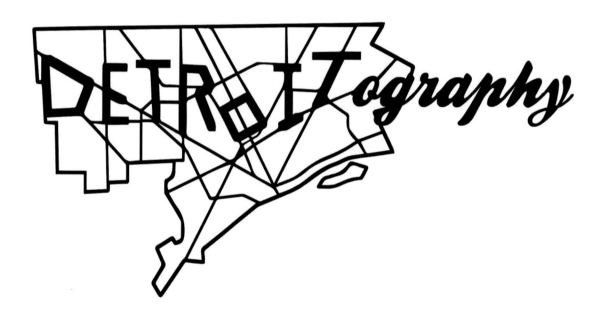

After living in Detroit for five years, I noticed that I had accumulated a handful of mapping projects in an effort to understand the city and my own place in it.

I launched DETROITography in 2013 to emphasize the unique way that people within the city think about space and place, their own idiosyncratic demographics and pathways and memories. My goal was to offer an array of insights as to the exact location of Detroit embedded within history but that would also be transformative related to dominant narratives of the city.

DETROITography has since grown to include a workshop series, regular mapping events, new job opportunities, and book publications.

This book is a reflection of more than a decade of effort to comprehend Detroit through its past, present, and people. The maps included here mirror the requests, needs, and questions of numerous Detroiters that I have been fortunate to have met and worked with.

There is a power in maps that can never be taken lightly.

—Alex B. Hill

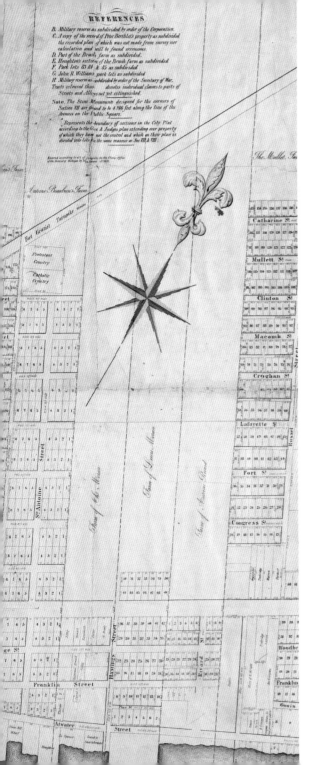

Before you dive in and begin answering questions about Detroit you never thought to ask, a disclaimer: this book should really be called *Detroit in (About) 50 Maps*. Depending on what you count as "one" map, there are between fifty and one hundred maps in the pages that follow, exploring the history, demographics, and culture of a great Midwestern city. But as I said at the beginning of *Cleveland in 50 Maps*, fifty is a nice round number, so we're going with that.

—Dan Crissman

# INTRODUCTION

Detroit is an easy city to map, but it is difficult to draw and even more difficult to navigate.

To truly understand the city is to comb through its layers. Some of those layers are historical, some are physical, and most are cultural. Thankfully, there is good food too.

To know Detroit, you have to ride the bus, enjoy gas station culinary creations, and make countless wrong turns. Most importantly, you have to listen. Detroit and Detroiters will tell you all about the city if you do.

Detroit is an amalgam of history: racism and redevelopment, cooperation and corporatism. It is a city laden with old and new opportunities constantly at odds. Plans from the 1970s come to fruition in the 2010s, and new ideas in the 2000s likely won't see the light of day for another fifty years.

Detroit is a juxtaposition of every known human (and animal) emotion and then some. It is a joy to travel the city's streets and a celebration to explore its communities.

Mound
Schoenherr
State Fair
Conant
Ryan
Dequindre
Davison
Hayes
Moross
Whittier
Conner
Gratiot
Harper
Van Dyke
Chandler
Alter
Grand Blvd
Mack
Forest
Mt. Elliott
Jefferson
Forest
Belle Isle

**Detroit is a significant city:** historically, economically, and spatially. Detroit is the oldest city settled in the Midwest and has had far-reaching influence as a center for trade, technological innovation, and community building. Detroit sits primarily on flat land made up of nondescript, sandy and gravelly soil that drains poorly. The land was nearly all forests and swamp. Most of the historical rivers and creeks have been covered over to serve as sewage drains. At the same time, the Detroit River is a primary freshwater source delivered by Detroit's water system to the four million or so people of the southeast Michigan region.

Detroit has held many titles and honorifics throughout its history. Many reflected the city's achievements, like Arsenal of Democracy or Hockey Town, while others reflected its crises, such as Murder City.

By population, Detroit is the largest city in Michigan with no other comparable cities in the state. Historically, that meant that Detroit had outsized political influence compared to other municipalities. The city population peaked in 1950 at nearly 1.8 million people. Detroit was known as America's "Fourth City" based on population.

Today, that political influence is diminished by the city's deep financial problems. It has the dubious distinction of being the largest municipal bankruptcy in the country, estimated in 2013 to be $17 billion.

The city also has some of the highest poverty rates and lowest job numbers in the country. Like other Rust Belt cities, loss of industry over the past several decades has been debilitating. Detroit's "Big 3" automakers no longer produce any vehicles in the city, and its last major automotive plant is now internationally owned.

In the twenty-first century, tax foreclosure by the Wayne County treasurer, compounded by subprime mortgage lending that targeted Black homeowners with faulty mortgages, caused many to lose their homes. High vacancy rates can still be found across the city.

Currently, Detroit is not well represented in national databases of neighborhood and retail amenities. This could be due to the high rate of population loss that was preceded by industry and retail flight from the city. The absence of national or chain retailers has left gaps in communities and datasets to represent the opportunities across the city.

Yet, Detroiters have endured. They have made their own food systems, built their own cooperatives, established numerous business and entrepreneurship incubators, and made a way out of no way. Resilience is an understatement in Detroit.

The maps included in this book seek to highlight the ways that Detroiters have made their own way, created their own coffee shops when Starbucks didn't care to, or grown their own food when stores didn't care to enter the city limits.

The maps in this book are divided into four sections.

The first section, "Situating the City," explores how Detroit compares to other large cities in the United States as well as some of the oddities and geographic nuances of place in the city. Maps of land annexation, investment zones, and pheasant populations hopefully give you a sense of what to expect.

The second section, "Getting to Know the City," takes you on a whirlwind tour of how to get around Detroit as well as some interesting differences in its demographics. Maps of the age of buildings, chronic dis-

ease, and elections give a sense of what makes up the city.

The third section, "Communities and Neighborhoods" takes you into the fraught territory of neighborhood naming and boundaries in the city. Responses from residents are mapped in various ways to counter what local government might define.

The final section, "Places in the City," catalogues the old, new, and unique places to visit, eat food, and meet other people.

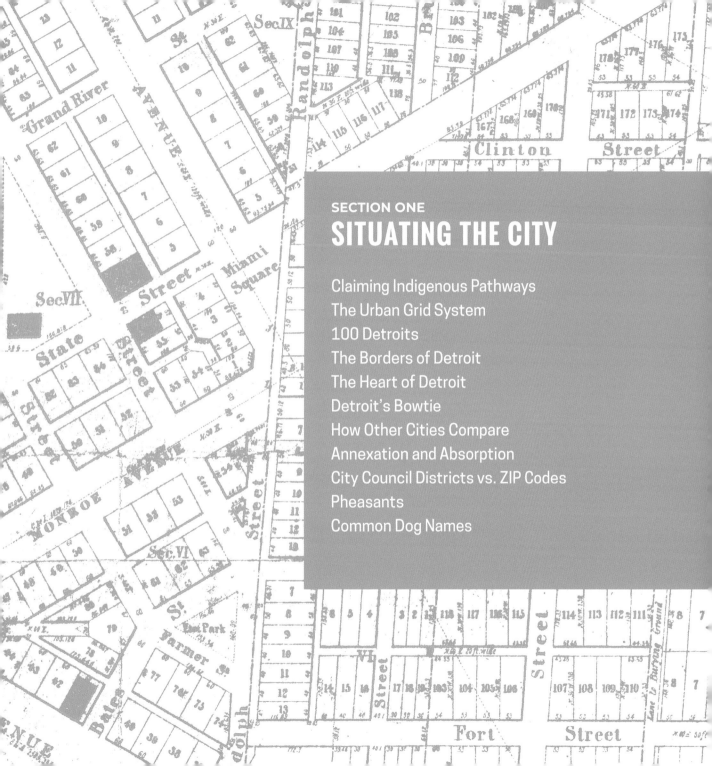

**SECTION ONE**

# SITUATING THE CITY

Claiming Indigenous Pathways
The Urban Grid System
100 Detroits
The Borders of Detroit
The Heart of Detroit
Detroit's Bowtie
How Other Cities Compare
Annexation and Absorption
City Council Districts vs. ZIP Codes
Pheasants
Common Dog Names

Palmer

Woodward

Grand River

Gratiot

Chandler

Rouge
Park

Jefferson

Belle
Isle

# CLAIMING INDIGENOUS PATHWAYS

Before the modern era, the people who inhabited or visited Detroit all had names related to the connective waterway that we call the Detroit River. Detroit's indigenous peoples named this place for the water because of its abundance, the life-giving ecosystems it supported, and the opportunities

it provided. The French colonizers in 1701 saw a similar waterway but focused on its strategic military advantage for controlling access to land and opportunity.

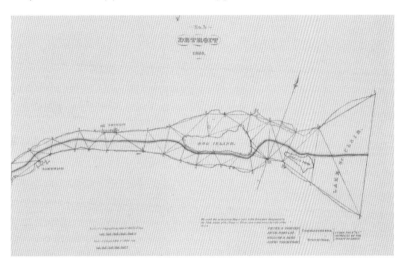

The city's current layout bears the mark of all of its past residents. Many note Detroit's growth and development after the Great Fire of 1805 as being modeled after French urban planning. The hub-and-spoke street layout drafted by Augustus Woodward is said to have been inspired by the plans of Paris and Washington, DC. Yet, the city's main arterial roadways claim the existing indigenous trails and pathways established in a time before any European land conquests.

# THE URBAN GRID SYSTEM

Detroit is a city of three distinct street grids.

Building upon indigenous travel and trading routes, the French influence can be seen with a focus on roadways that move up and away from the riverfront, creating a long and rectangular coastal grid. The proposed 10,000-acre plot centered on Highland Park extended the French angles while introducing a standard grid.

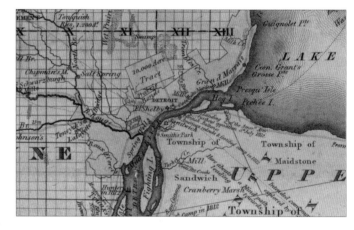

The Jeffersonian one-square-mile grid system, implemented as part of the 1785 Land Ordinance, was applied after American control was finalized, giving Detroit and its region its distinct mile road system.

The city's last great road system was the expressways. Detroit boasts the first segment of paved roadway ever placed, and its expressway system grew exponentially once it got started, cutting through Detroit's Black communities. Thankfully, the number of expressways built was lower than what was included in early proposals.

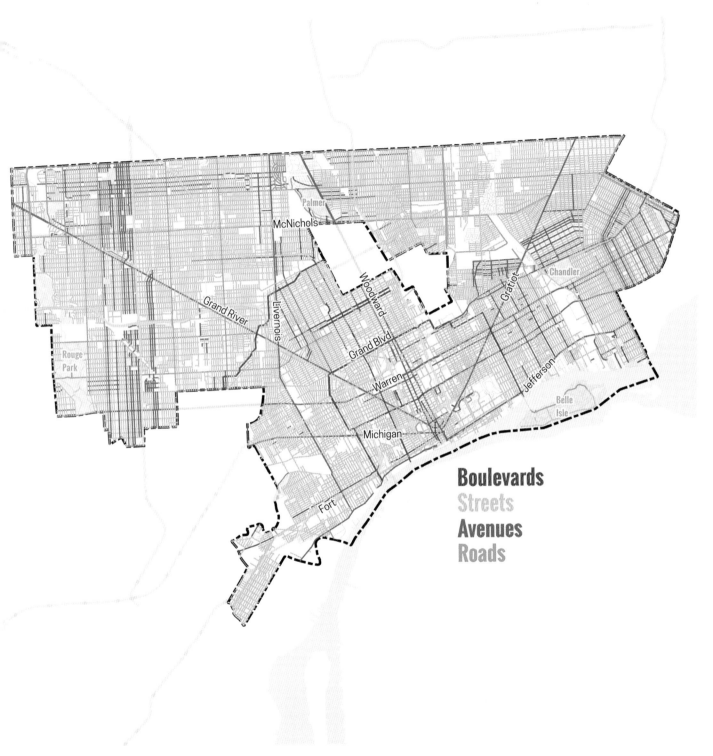

Palmer

McNichols

Woodward

Grand River

Livernois

Chandler

Gratiot

Grand Blvd

Warren

Jefferson

Belle
Isle

Rouge
Park

Michigan

Fort

**Boulevards**
Streets
**Avenues**
Roads

Palmer
McNichols
Woodward
Chandler
Grand River
Gratiot
Livernois
Rouge Park
Grand Blvd
Warren
Jefferson
Belle Isle
Michigan
Fort

## STREETS OF DETROIT

As evidenced by all the yellow on the map, the term "street" was used widely in all three of Detroit's urban grid systems. It's hard to go anywhere in the city and not drive on a street.

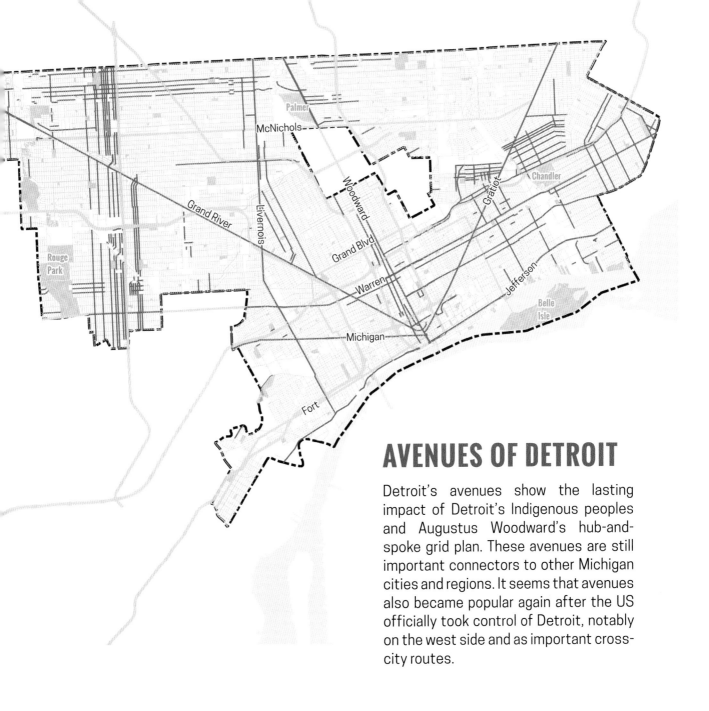

# AVENUES OF DETROIT

Detroit's avenues show the lasting impact of Detroit's Indigenous peoples and Augustus Woodward's hub-and-spoke grid plan. These avenues are still important connectors to other Michigan cities and regions. It seems that avenues also became popular again after the US officially took control of Detroit, notably on the west side and as important cross-city routes.

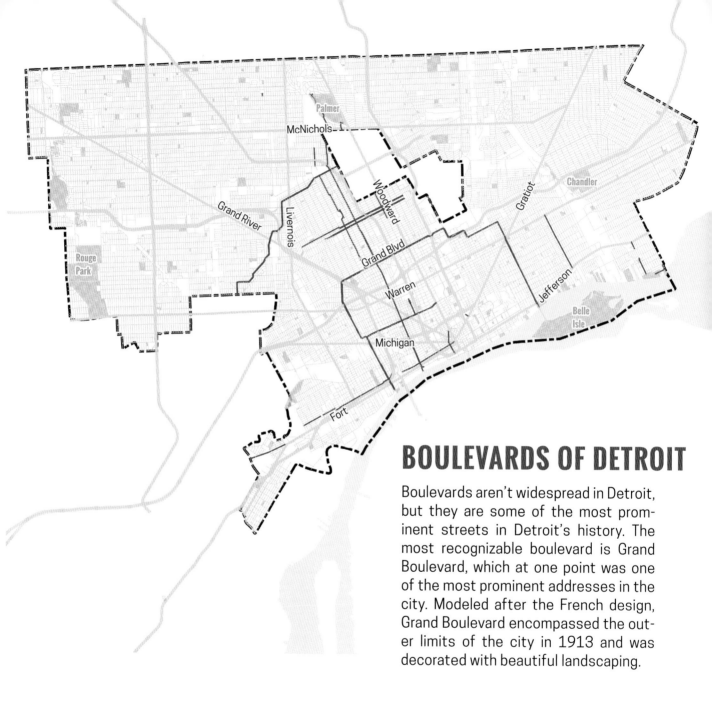

# BOULEVARDS OF DETROIT

Boulevards aren't widespread in Detroit, but they are some of the most prominent streets in Detroit's history. The most recognizable boulevard is Grand Boulevard, which at one point was one of the most prominent addresses in the city. Modeled after the French design, Grand Boulevard encompassed the outer limits of the city in 1913 and was decorated with beautiful landscaping.

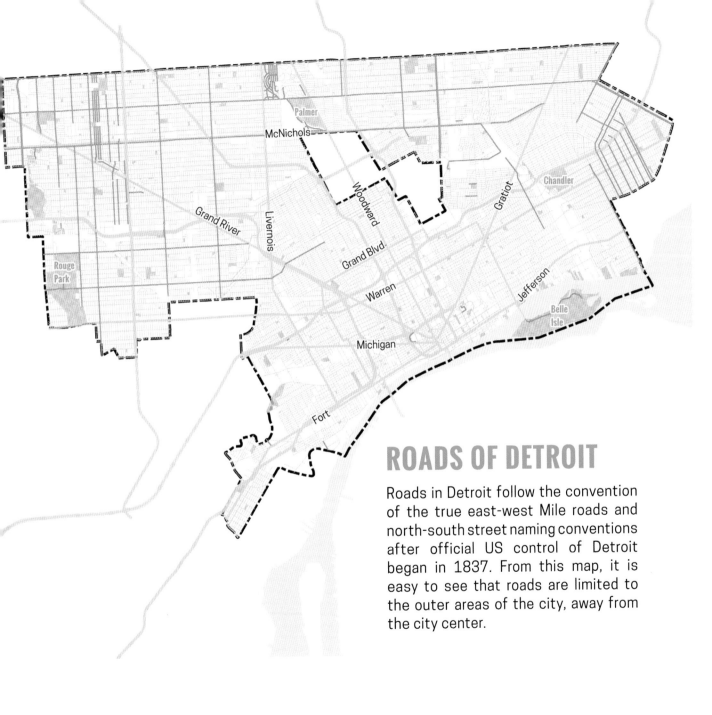

## ROADS OF DETROIT

Roads in Detroit follow the convention of the true east-west Mile roads and north-south street naming conventions after official US control of Detroit began in 1837. From this map, it is easy to see that roads are limited to the outer areas of the city, away from the city center.

# The "Map of Detroit" 100

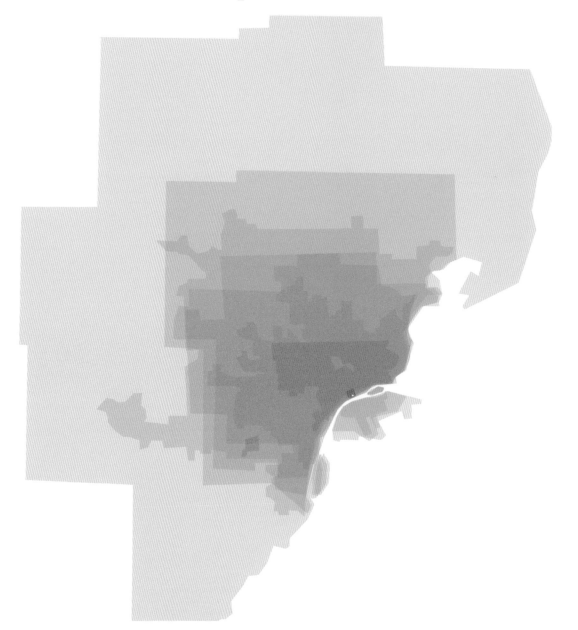

# 100 DETROITS

As much as Detroit is a very specific place, it is also a broad idea and imagined space.

In 2013, Yale historian Bill Rankin published a map that looked at the Midwest as defined by 100 different corporations, organizations, and agencies. The boundaries of the Midwest are not agreed upon, and so too goes the geographic definition of "Detroit." The term means many different things to different people. Most importantly, the city's name is claimed by people spread across an expansive region.

To explore the geography of what people mean when they say "Detroit," the first 100 images that appeared in a Google image search for "map of Detroit" have been overlaid and merged in the map on the left.

A number of the 100 maps show urban sprawl to varying degrees, while some maps categorize municipalities around the city as "Detroit." Some maps even included parts of Windsor, Ontario, in the "metro Detroit" area. The larger boundaries match the Combined Statistical Area (CSA) and the Metropolitan Statistical Area (MSA) as outlined by the federal Office of Management and Budget (OMB), which represent "Detroit" as either a 6-county area (MSA) or a 9-county area (CSA).

Many corporations based in Southfield, Warren, or Dearborn choose to say they are based in "Detroit" due to their proximity and airport designation. However, even the Detroit Metropolitan Airport is located in Romulus, not Detroit. Most regional organizations (Detroit Chamber, Detroit Water & Sewerage, SEMCOG, and others) represent Detroit with boundaries that extend into surrounding municipalities, most commonly the tri-counties (Wayne, Oakland, and Ma-

# The Borders of Detroit

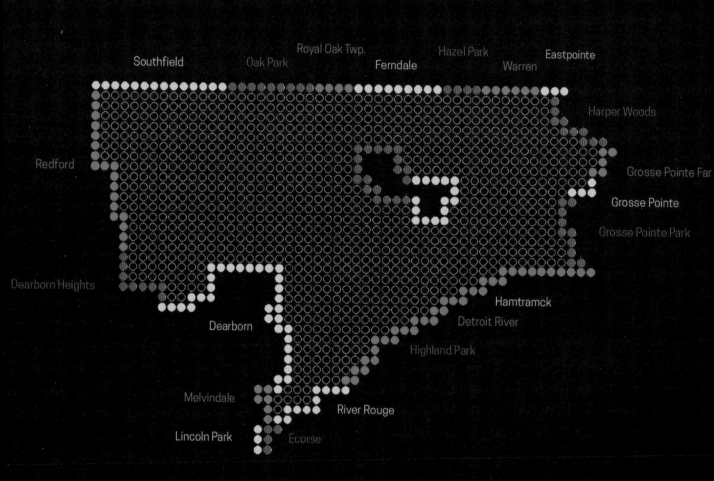

Southfield

Oak Park

Royal Oak Twp.

Ferndale

Hazel Park

Warren

Eastpointe

Harper Woods

Redford

Grosse Pointe Far

Grosse Pointe

Grosse Pointe Park

Dearborn Heights

Dearborn

Hamtramck

Detroit River

Highland Park

Melvindale

River Rouge

Lincoln Park

Ecorse

Living in the city of Detroit or its metro area, it is easy to get confused by all of the neighboring municipalities. This map highlights the various borders that surround the city and define its limits.

Detroit is bordered by twenty separate municipalities and one river. The Detroit River has the longest border with the city, followed by the city of Dearborn. The metropolitan region's history is one marked by land annexation and home rule. The home rule policy allowed people to band together in smaller municipalities in order to stave off annexation by Detroit.

The existence of the home rule policy has led to a fractured region that reflects its racial and economic disparities. Southfield became a Black middle-class enclave. Warren remains a city with a reputation as being unfriendly toward Black people. Dearborn now exists as a city with the highest concentration of people of Arab descent outside of the Middle East.

# THE HEART OF DETROIT

The "heart of Detroit" is a common marketing shtick, attempting to show the importance and purported hipness of a given location. Sometimes that location is a new development. At other times it is a historic place marker.

But can we determine the true "heart" or center? Thanks to Aaron Foley's 2012 article on this very topic and some more recent Google searches, we can assemble a list of locations assumed to be the "heart of Detroit" that have a wide geographic variation.

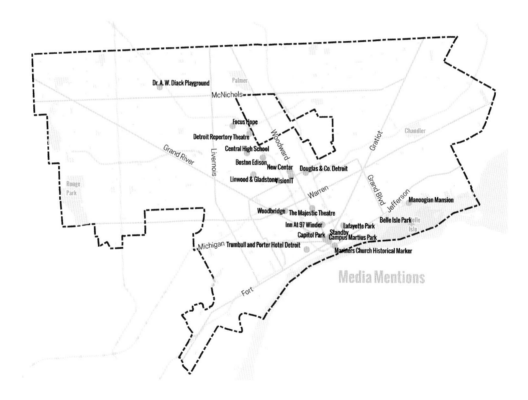

Media mentions are nice, and the geographic center is helpful, but it is no mystery that Detroit is a very large area with random clusters of population.

Using more math, we can calculate the mean "center of population" for Detroit. It seems that the "inner cartographer" of Aaron Foley (author of *The Detroit Neighborhood Guidebook* and *How to Live in Detroit Without Being a Jackass*) was spot on!

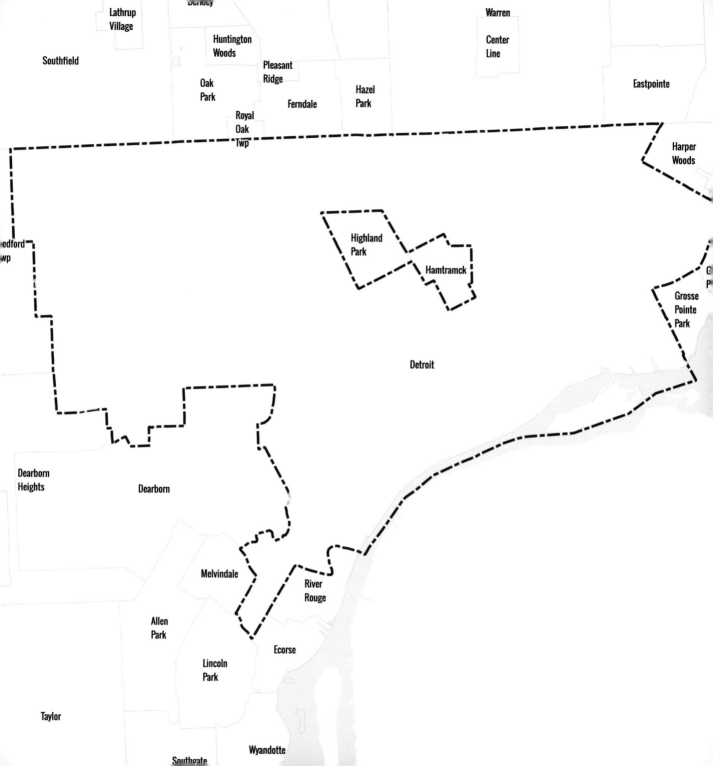

# DETROIT'S BOWTIE

Detroit is never alone and is always dressed up. Encompassed within Detroit's city limits are the city of Highland Park and the city of Hamtramck, which together form a bowtie shape just above the "heart" of the city.

Highland Park is best known as the original headquarters for the Ford Motor Company, whose Model T factory was located there.

Hamtramck is historically known for its large Polish population and paczki donuts.

In many maps of Detroit, these cities are left blank. Sometimes that is due to a lack of data or information. Sometimes that is due to haste and mapmaking laziness.

boston

new york

washington d.c.

san francisco

charlotte

el paso

baltimore

memphis

seattle

denver

milwaukee

las vegas

philadelphia

atlanta

mesa

portland

# HOW OTHER CITIES COMPARE

Can Detroit really be compared to any other city? Many have tried comparing crime rates, the economy, and poverty levels in Detroit with other troubled cities. A few groups have even tried fitting different city land areas into Detroit's 139 square (land) miles. It always seems that Detroit has too much or too little of something for a city-to-city comparison to make much sense.

In this map series, Detroit is compared with sixteen other large cities by land mass, population density, and population size. Common comparisons include the popular comparison map (Boston, New York City, Washington, DC, San Francisco), similar population sizes (Charlotte, El Paso, Baltimore, Memphis), similar population density (Seattle, Denver, Milwaukee, Las Vegas) and similar land sizes (Philadelphia, Atlanta, Mesa, Portland).

The 2010 census population for Detroit was 713,777, closer to San Francisco's. Imagine San Francisco's southern edge lined up with the riverfront and perhaps we can see what proponents of a "condensed" city envision. Should the city condense to its former 1913 borders and focus on making services work within that area before moving outward? Or would that just be an exercise in discrimination and inequality?

While there is still no great comparison city for Detroit, looking at how the city matches up with many of its comparison cities is an important exercise.

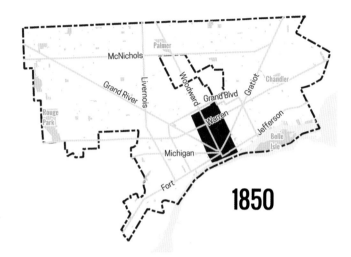

**1850**

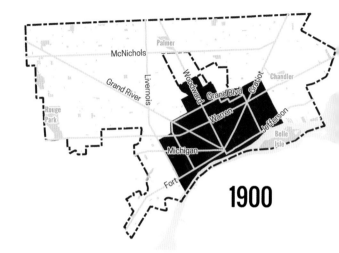

**1900**

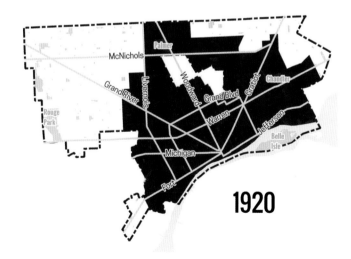

**1920**

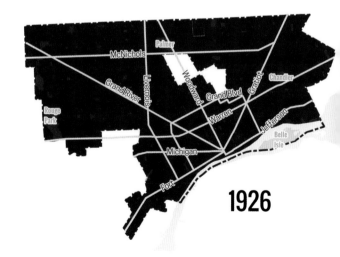

**1926**

# ANNEXATION AND ABSORPTION

You can learn a lot about Detroit's history from its expansion over the years. Detroit's slivered expansion northward from the river is evident before the city began fanning out along the Detroit River's edge. The city's purchase of Belle Isle in 1879 added the largest island park in the country. The glory days of Grand Boulevard in 1891 show the city before it ever extend any further north. Finally, the rapid land acquisition in the 1920s expanded the city's land area as the auto industry boomed and population swelled.

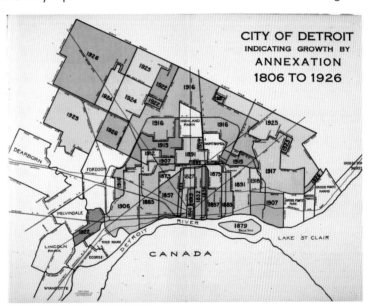

Detroit's industry, population, and services have changed drastically over the years, but the physical boundaries of the city have remained the same since 1926.

The 1947 Master Plan referred to the process as being "absorbed" by Detroit. Both annexation and absorption were topics of concern for communities in the region. Many formed their own small municipalities so that they couldn't be swallowed up by Detroit.

# CITY COUNCIL DISTRICTS VS. ZIP CODES

The lines in this map don't align.

One set of lines are zone improvement plan (ZIP) codes based off of postal delivery routes. The other set of lines are political designations. The US census doesn't collect data for either category. Yet residents and politicians both more readily recognize their ZIP code or council district before any other geographic area.

In 2009, the plan for district-based voting was passed by the city council. In 2012, Detroit extensively updated its city charter and city council elections to be based on the geographic council districts.

# PHEASANTS

Detroit's unofficial avian mascot is the Chinese ring-necked pheasant. The birds were brought to the west side of Michigan in 1895 and slowly made their way to Detroit via small farms across the state.

A pheasant encounter is a uniquely Detroit experience—whether walking a dog, driving on an almost vacant street, or viewing the waterfront by the Detroit River. Pheasants have thrived in Detroit's urban landscape.

Because of the uniqueness of sighting a pheasant, you can now find the bird emblazoned on a community soccer team jersey, a mural in Corktown, and a ceiling painting at the Red Hook coffee shop on the city's east side.

This pheasant map is a collection of mentions from any and all online media of pheasant sightings in Detroit and included the data from local public radio station, WDET's listener crowdsourcing of pheasant sightings in 2016.

The map includes 109 sightings of roughly 300 pheasants in Detroit between 2002 and 2016. Some sightings were likely the same pheasant seen over and over again while others were just a lone bird out looking for food beyond its normal range.

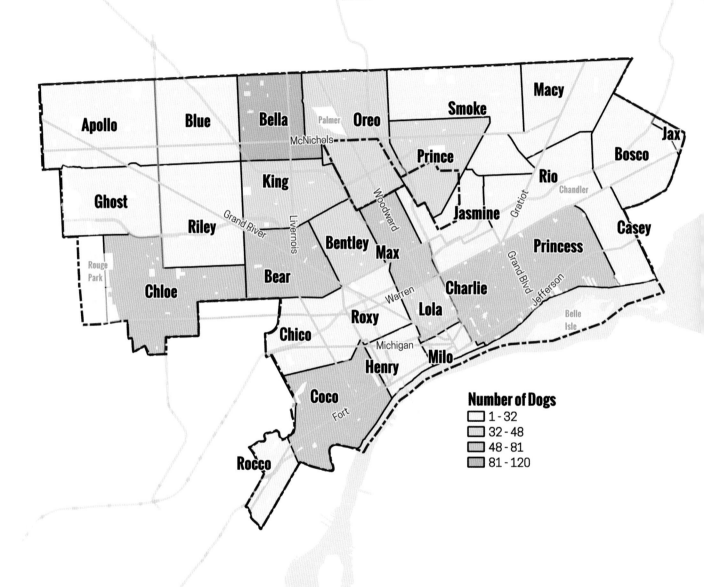

**Number of Dogs**
- 1 - 32
- 32 - 48
- 48 - 81
- 81 - 120

# COMMON DOG NAMES

Bella, Max, Charlie, and Coco. If you don't know these names yet, then you probably haven't met many dogs in Detroit.

When many people hear about dogs in Detroit, it's usually a terrible story about a dog attack or overblown claims of "packs of dogs" roaming the city streets. Detroit has plenty of stray dogs, and some travel in packs, but most of the city's canines live comfortably as beloved pets.

While every dog is supposed to be licensed with the city's animal care and control division, most aren't. The data for this map comes from the great team at Canine to Five, a dog boarding and grooming business in the city.

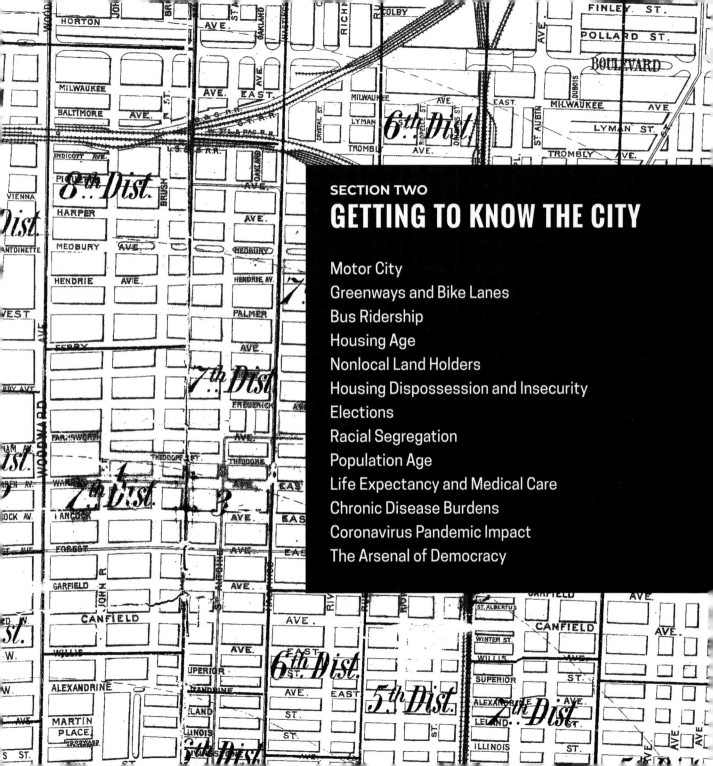

SECTION TWO
# GETTING TO KNOW THE CITY

Motor City
Greenways and Bike Lanes
Bus Ridership
Housing Age
Nonlocal Land Holders
Housing Dispossession and Insecurity
Elections
Racial Segregation
Population Age
Life Expectancy and Medical Care
Chronic Disease Burdens
Coronavirus Pandemic Impact
The Arsenal of Democracy

# MOTOR CITY

To navigate Detroit effectively you need to have access to a car.

Detroit is a city of roads. There isn't much else available for transportation yet. The city's bus system has been abhorrent for years, but it has renewed investment from the local and federal government. The bus system rebranded and launched the Connect Ten focus on their top 10 busiest routes to improve the frequency and reliability of buses.

Still, not everyone has access to a vehicle in Detroit. Households with no vehicle access make up over 25% of the city. Data that show 70% of all jobs in Detroit are held by those who commute into the city, typically by car. The city has prioritized commuters over residents in their transportation planning.

Households with No Vehicle

| 0 | 82 | 191 | 379 | 1,011 |

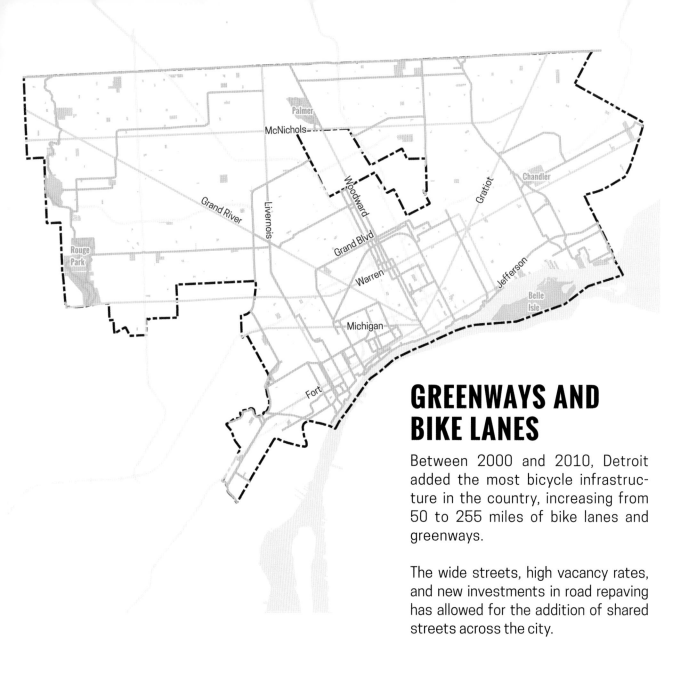

# GREENWAYS AND BIKE LANES

Between 2000 and 2010, Detroit added the most bicycle infrastructure in the country, increasing from 50 to 255 miles of bike lanes and greenways.

The wide streets, high vacancy rates, and new investments in road repaving has allowed for the addition of shared streets across the city.

# BUS RIDERSHIP

Detroit's public transit system is woefully inadequate for the city's size and relatively low density. But the DDOT still serves millions of riders every year.

The map above shows the most popular bus routes according to where people get on and off. More people ride the bus along Detroit's major arterial roadways as well as some of the crosstown routes along Warren, 7 Mile, and McNichols.

pre - 1900

1900 - 1950

1950 - 1980

1980 - present

# HOUSING AGE

The map on the left helps visually illustrate Detroit's three major booms and busts. As a frontier town at the center of water transportation and trade, the "Old City" is still visible. The post-World War II housing construction boom is evident as Detroit's population fled the dirty and factory-focused Downtown into essentially suburban neighborhoods. Finally, the new efforts at revitalization that have churned since the 1970s are evident in the newer construction surrounded by empty space.

Most of the newer construction has occurred in more vacant areas, which could also represent larger land parcels being reduced to a point location (i.e., a hospital). There is some very interesting clustering of pre-1930 and post-1970 construction in Midtown and Corktown. At least in construction, Old Detroit and New Detroit prefer to be closer together.

In the gradient near the bottom center, you can also spot the former area of Paradise Valley and Black Bottom, which have been largely vacant after being demolished in the 1950s and 1960s under the federal "urban renewal" program that focused on "slum clearance" and "blight reduction."

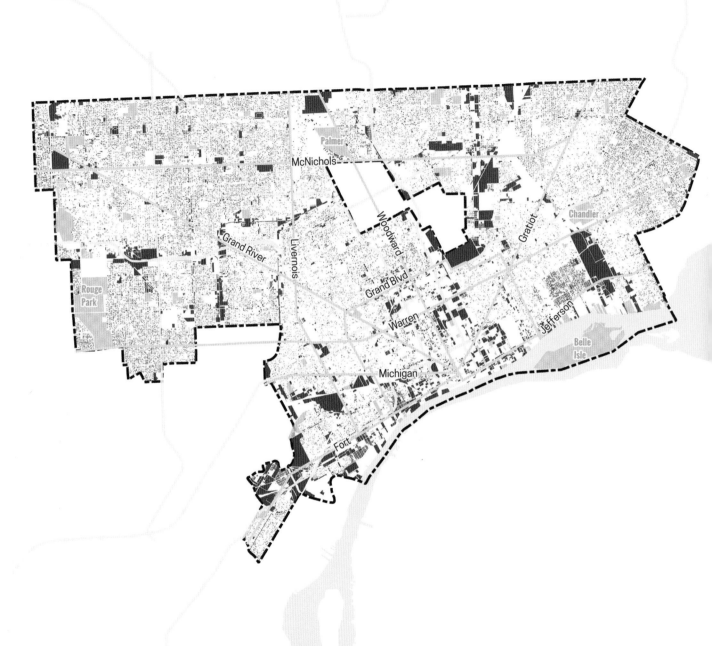

# NONLOCAL LAND HOLDERS

Detroit has been a city of change. Possibly the most significant change has been in land ownership. Detroit used to be a city of predominantly homeowners, but it is now more of a 50/50 split. Economic decline, tax foreclosure, subprime mortgage lending, and property speculation are just a few of the reasons why.

Detroit's city government owns about 30% of the land, including parks, public use areas like recreation centers and government offices, and vacant properties. Property speculators, or individuals who own more than five properties outside of the neighborhood where they live, own 20% of all properties.

In many neighborhoods, residents don't know who owns the vacant properties on their block. Speculative investments on vacant houses in Detroit has led to the further deterioration of communities, often beyond residents' control.

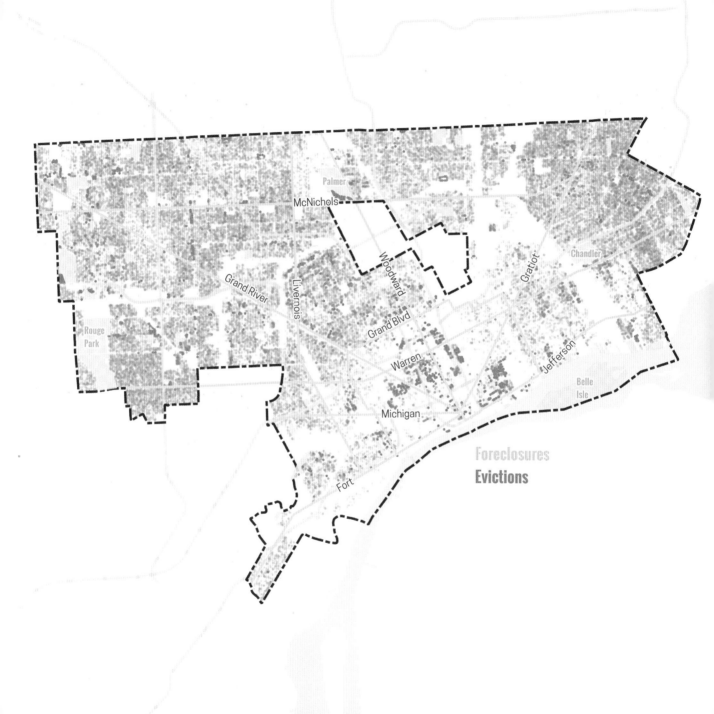

Palmer

McNichols

Woodward

Chandler

Gratiot

Grand River

Livernois

Rouge
Park

Grand Blvd

Warren

Jefferson

Belle
Isle

Michigan

Foreclosures
**Evictions**

Fort

# HOUSING DISPOSSESSION AND INSECURITY

There is a common narrative in the media that Detroit is empty, a blank canvas where anything can be done, especially as it relates to homes. This false narrative doesn't account for the nearly 700,000 people who already live in the city.

Most Detroiters live in the precarious spot of having a steady but insufficient income. They live in a home, but they're unsure if they'll be able to make rent or cover utilities and groceries each month. The United Way classifies these households as "asset-limited, income-constrained, employed," or ALICE. In Detroit, nearly 70% of all households fall into this category.

# ELECTIONS

Detroiters do not vote in large numbers. During a presidential election, close to half of all voters in the city participate. For mayoral elections, the city is lucky to see over 20% of voters participate.

The city of Detroit, after the labor movement took hold, has long been a Democratic stronghold. That doesn't mean that Detroit's politics have been staid and predictable. There have been frightening moments in its history, such as when a mayoral candidate won by write-in support from the Ku Klux Klan. There has also been plenty of political scandal, most prominently during Mayor Kwame Kilpatrick's term (2002–2008).

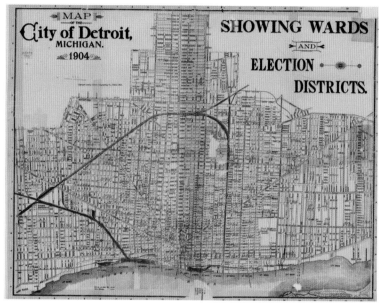

It's likely that the breakdown of politics over the years, the difficulty of finding one's polling places on Election Day, and the lack of trust in politicians has stifled Detroiters' voting turnout recently.

Voter turnout for Obama's 2008 election was 53%. The rate of voter turnout has decreased ever since with almost 49% of eligible voters casting a ballot in 2016.

Mayor Mike Duggan has won election twice with less about 25% of eligible voters casting a ballot both times. He won in 2013, with less than 20% of voters participating, and again in 2017, when the rate of voters reached just 21%.

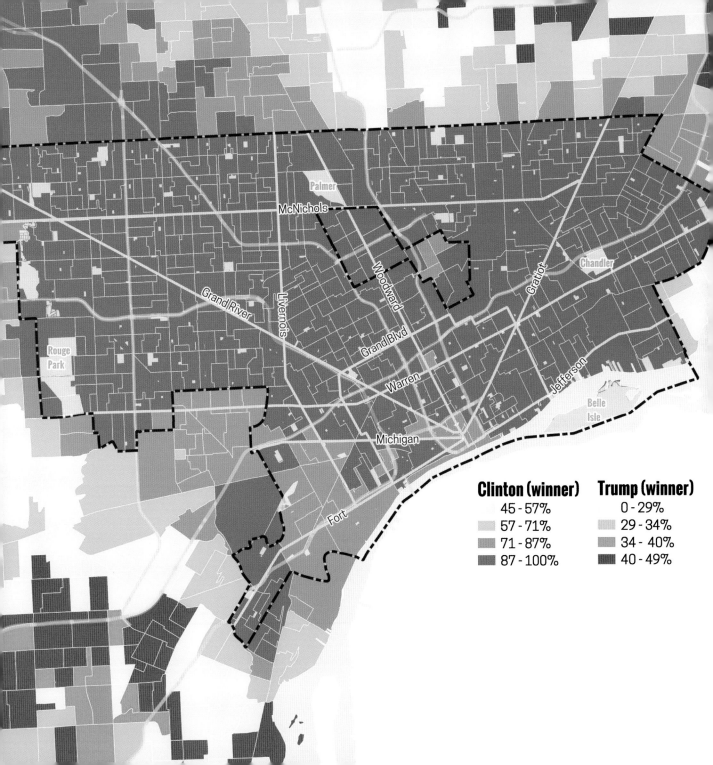

Palmer

McNichols

Woodward

Chandler

Gratiot

Grand River

Livernois

Grand Blvd

Rouge
Park

Warren

Jefferson

Belle
Isle

Michigan

Fort

**Clinton (winner)**
45 - 57%
57 - 71%
71 - 87%
87 - 100%

**Trump (winner)**
0 - 29%
29 - 34%
34 - 40%
40 - 49%

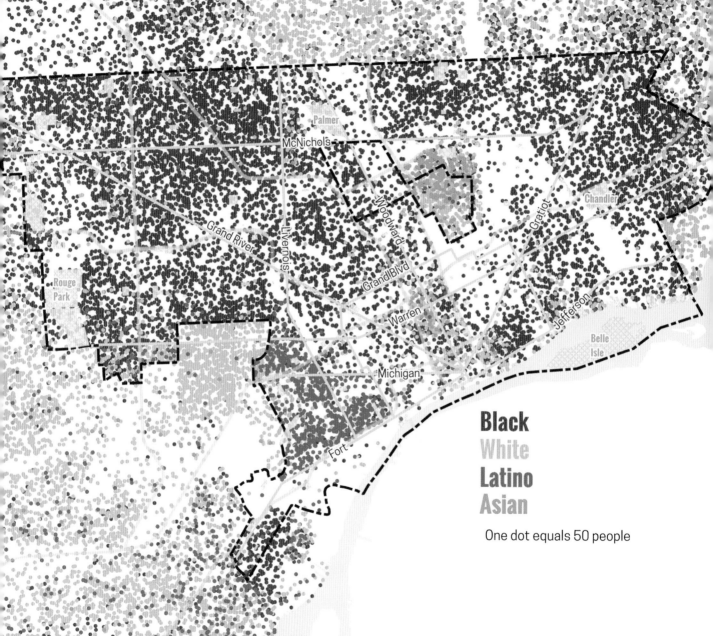

Palmer

McNichols

Woodward

Chandler

Grand River

Livernois

Gratiot

Grand Blvd

Rouge Park

Warren

Jefferson

Belle Isle

Michigan

Fort

**Black**
White
**Latino**
Asian

One dot equals 50 people

# RACIAL SEGREGATION

In 2019, *USA Today* listed Detroit again in the 25 "most segregated" cities in America. In truth, Detroit is a homogeneous city—almost 80% Black—situated in a deeply divided region that is split across many political boundaries. There are a number of growing immigrant populations in and around Hamtramck, but by and large, Detroit and its metro region have remained mostly the same since 2000. You can see the more recent "Black flight" (26% population loss in Detroit between 2000 and 2010) in the top left corner of the city into the nearby suburb of Southfield.

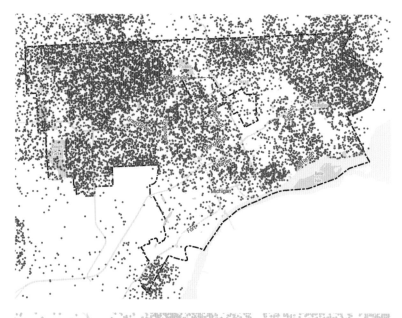

**BLACK POPULATION**

**WHITE POPULATION**

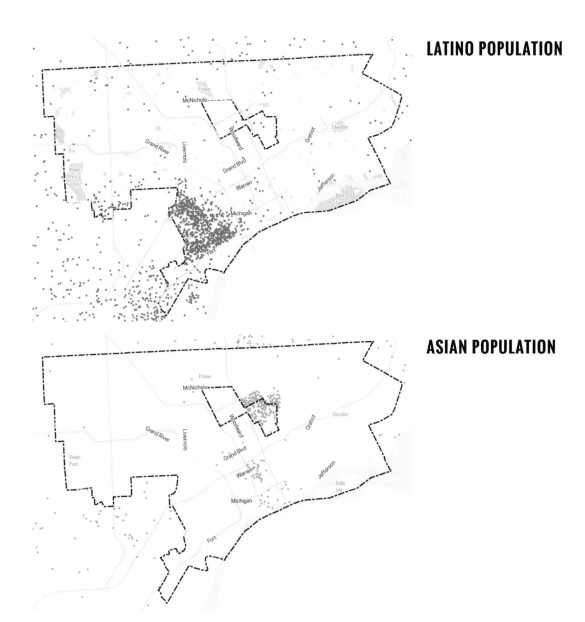

LATINO POPULATION

ASIAN POPULATION

More Children (under Age 17)
More Elderly (Age 65+)

# POPULATION AGE

Detroit's greatest challenge is to better serve its children while at the same time taking care of its elderly. Far too many Detroiters of both populations suffer an early death from preventable causes.

The age balance or imbalance across the geography of Detroit results in some interesting areas where children or the elderly make up a majority of the population. Not surprisingly, many of the areas with the most children also have fewer elderly residents. The riverfront has a larger elderly population due to the senior apartment high-rises located there. Grand River cuts an interesting pattern along the west side, where there are more elderly above the avenue and more children below.

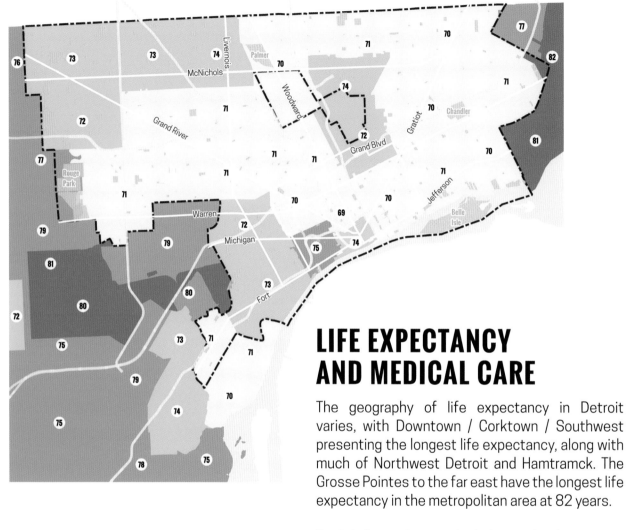

# LIFE EXPECTANCY AND MEDICAL CARE

The geography of life expectancy in Detroit varies, with Downtown / Corktown / Southwest presenting the longest life expectancy, along with much of Northwest Detroit and Hamtramck. The Grosse Pointes to the far east have the longest life expectancy in the metropolitan area at 82 years.

Social determinants, including school systems, health facility availability, and access to various opportunities that are lacking in the city, are also influential factors.

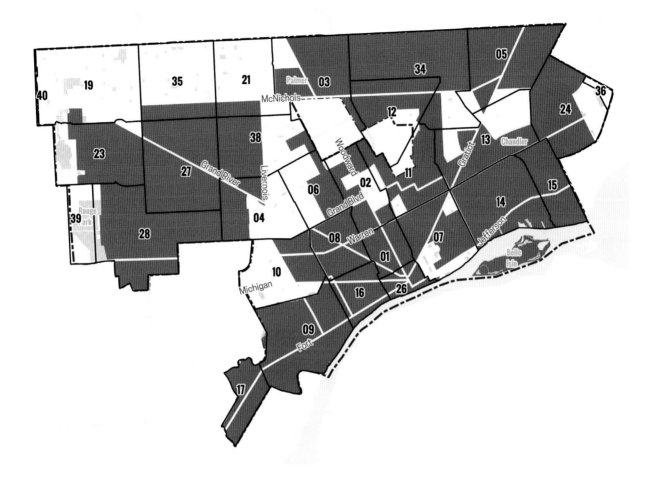

Detroit is a city where nearly 70% of the population lives in a medically underserved area, which means that access to a doctor is difficult and the mortality rate is high. Detroiters are not well served by the local health system, and as a result, life expectancy is lower.

# CHRONIC DISEASE BURDENS

Health conditions and diseases like obesity, diabetes, and heart disease can lead to health complications and untimely death. The disastrous impact of poor diet on our health is widely known, and yet still underestimated.

Detroit's obesity rate also ranked highest among other large metropolitan areas. The city has some of the highest rates in the country for chronic disease, appearing in the top ten out of 500 cities for obesity (#2), heart disease (#10), and diabetes (#2).

**Obesity Prevalence among Adults**

26     43     46     48     53%

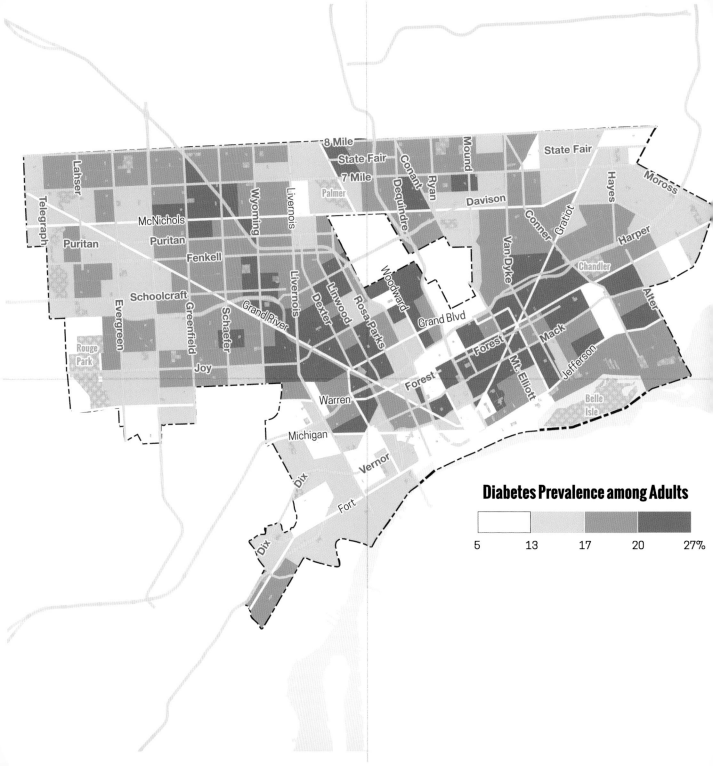

**Diabetes Prevalence among Adults**

| | | | | |
|---|---|---|---|---|
| 5 | 13 | 17 | 20 | 27% |

**Asthma Prevalence among Adults**

9   12   13   14   16%

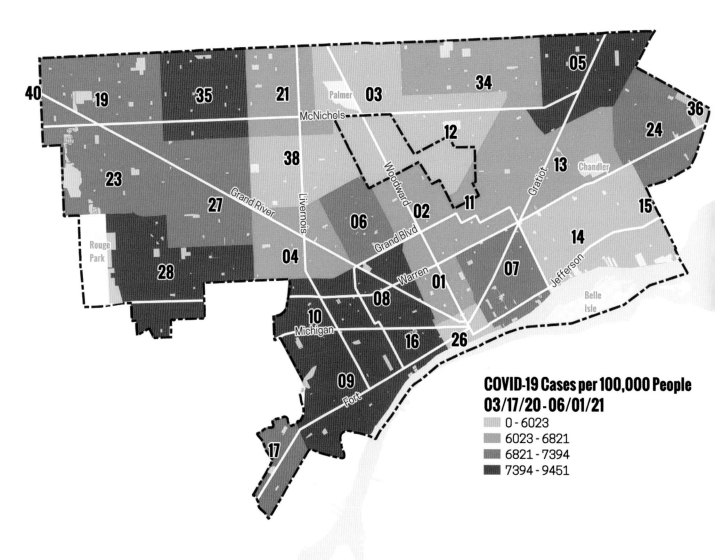

**COVID-19 Cases per 100,000 People
03/17/20 - 06/01/21**

- 0 - 6023
- 6023 - 6821
- 6821 - 7394
- 7394 - 9451

# CORONAVIRUS PANDEMIC IMPACT

Metro Detroit was a hotspot for the coronavirus pandemic, and COVID-19 cases regularly spiked across the region. As part of the pandemic response, foreclosure and water shutoffs were halted in order to reduce the impact on residents facing even greater uncertainty from the virus.

A March 2020 community breakfast hosted by the Detroit police department became the first documented transmission of COVID-19 within the general city population. By the end of March 2020, almost 70 Detroit police officers were infected as well as 8 members of the Detroit fire department.

In April, the city council president tested positive, and the nursing staff at Sinai-Grace Hospital staged a walkout over desperate conditions at the hospital. The mayor announced that almost 3,000 employees would be furloughed in the same month. Public data tracking of confirmed cases began.

Following the spring 2020 spike in cases, Detroit experienced another spike in November around the holidays. The biggest spike of the entire pandemic, however, occurred in April 2021 as restrictions were lifted and people wanted to enjoy the spring.

The city's testing and vaccination response followed a slow rollout similar to the government's efforts throughout the state. Glaring disparities in access to care and vaccination remained. Mobile health units became a regular tool to get access and care to communities in need. The Wayne Health group along with ACCESS, Henry Ford Health System, and the Detroit Health Department all coordinated mobile health units across the city.

# THE ARSENAL OF DEMOCRACY

During both World Wars, Detroit's factories and their manufacturing might was flipped from automobile production to support for the war effort. The green dots in the map above reflect the more than 100 factories in Detroit that were retooled to produce parts for aircraft, tanks, and weapons.

Recently, the news media have reached back into history in an attempt to compare the global coronavirus pandemic to a war effort. While there are serious issues with comparing a public health response to a war, the comparison fails on its own terms because Detroit no longer has an arsenal from which to pull. There are no longer over 100 factories within the city limits. The auto industry's operations are no longer located in Detroit.

The return of distilleries and breweries in Detroit has led to the city's strongest response; Detroit-based breweries and distilleries mass-produced hand sanitizer rather than beer or spirits. Detroit's industrial sewing ecosystem has also taken on the task of making face shields, gowns, and masks.

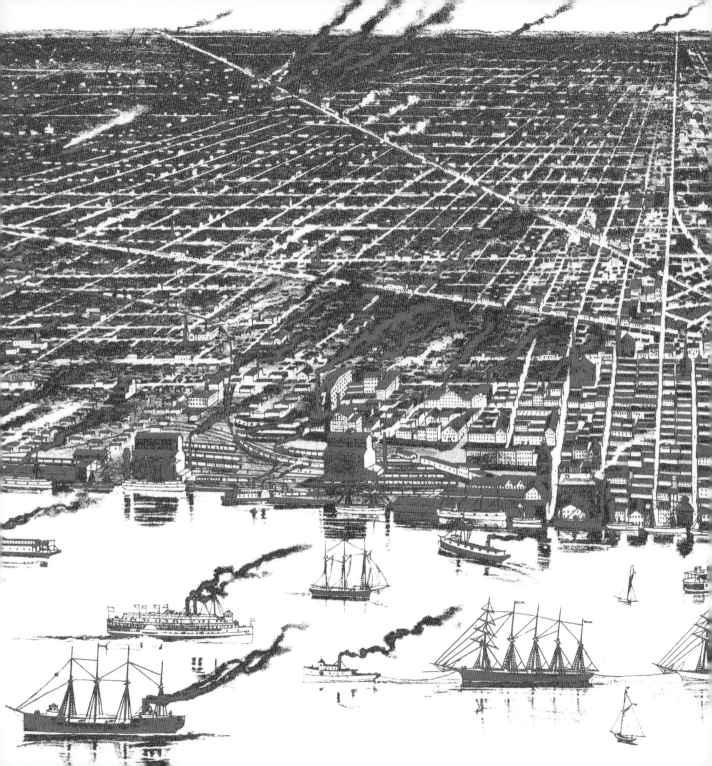

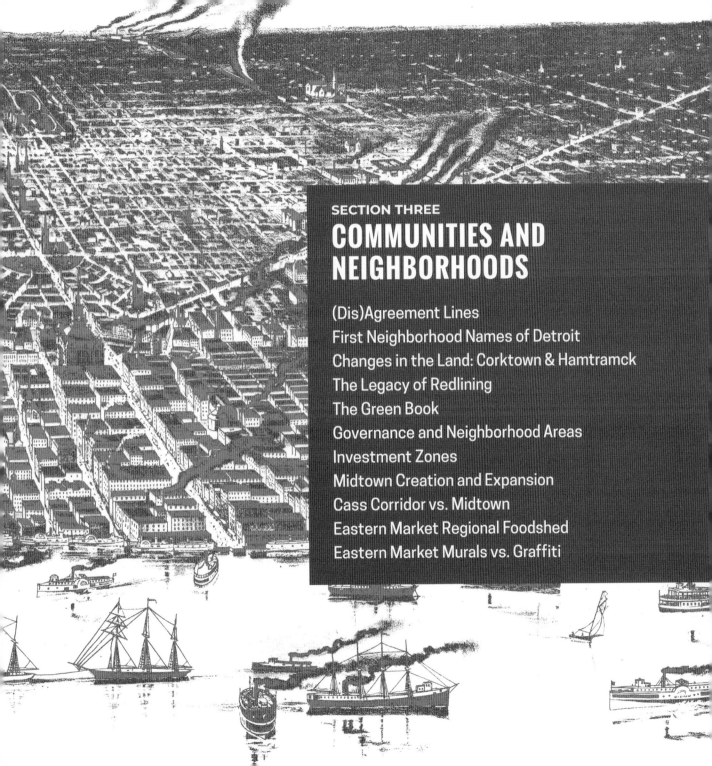

SECTION THREE

# COMMUNITIES AND NEIGHBORHOODS

(Dis)Agreement Lines
First Neighborhood Names of Detroit
Changes in the Land: Corktown & Hamtramck
The Legacy of Redlining
The Green Book
Governance and Neighborhood Areas
Investment Zones
Midtown Creation and Expansion
Cass Corridor vs. Midtown
Eastern Market Regional Foodshed
Eastern Market Murals vs. Graffiti

# (DIS)AGREEMENT LINES

Detroit neighborhoods are far from being well-known or agreed upon. Boundary lines get drawn and redrawn as new leaders take office or new initiatives get funded. Occasionally, that means that neighborhoods get redrawn or redefined.

The City of Detroit Master Plan of 1941 breaks the city apart into very specific "neighborhoods" based on the availability of a specific collection of places: a school, a park, and a certain amount of residential housing. However, that time period was also when the city's population was nearly 2 million people.

In recent years, Detroit has been more malleable to the interests of whomever had not left. Now monied interests and a local government hoping to recoup past losses hope to cash in on naming the city.

The featured map is a compilation of user-submitted neighborhoods (Loveland Technologies, n=129), Zillow neighborhoods, and the City of Detroit Master Plan neighborhoods. The brighter lines represent more agreement, while the lighter lines represent less agreement. Even from this map, we can see neighborhoods that are obviously recognizable. This map also highlights the areas of Detroit that don't have strong neighborhood identities. Hopefully, more community engagement will help neighborhoods and communities to develop their own sense of identity and naming as Detroit welcomes new investments and new residents.

# FIRST NEIGHBORHOOD NAMES OF DETROIT

These area names come from *The History of Detroit and Michigan* by Detroit's first cartographer, Silas Farmer, in 1884. Many of these names remain, with Corktown likely being the most recognizable. The development of the expressways changed the Corktown neighborhood, but the neighborhood was not totally wiped off the map like Kentucky along Hastings Street, which does not exist today.

Dutchtown isn't much referred to today, but Germantown Park (Harmonie Park) can still be visited Downtown. Polacktown seems to have morphed into Poletown, but the Polish population has mostly moved to Hamtramck. Piety Hill, named for the wealthy families and churches, is a name now associated with an entirely different section of the city.

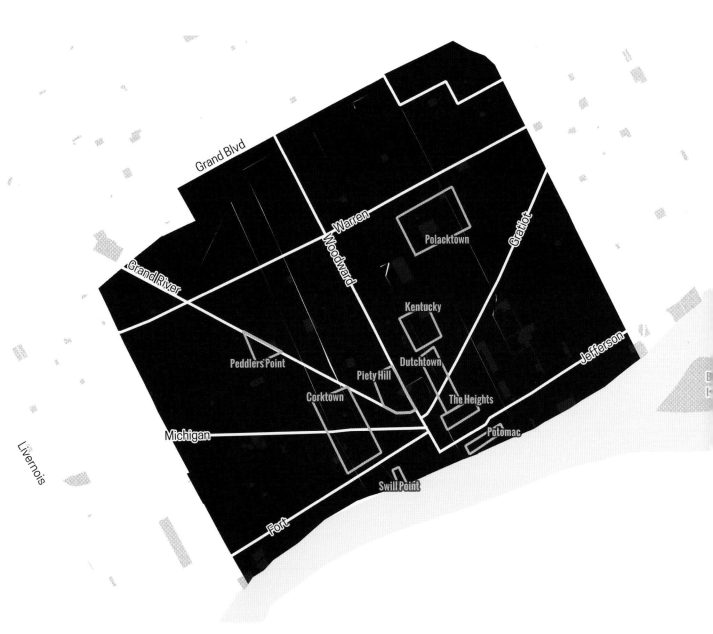

Grand Blvd

Warren

Woodward

Grand River

Gratiot

Polacktown

Kentucky

Peddlers Point

Dutchtown

Piety Hill

Jefferson

Corktown

The Heights

Michigan

Potomac

Livernois

Swill Point

Fort

# CHANGES IN THE LAND: CORKTOWN

Corktown may be Detroit's "oldest" neighborhood, but what we call Corktown today is very different than it once was.

Just as Detroit does not end at the city limits, neighborhoods and communities in Detroit are rarely definitively bounded areas unless there is a strong economic interest involved. We can see this idea of evolving boundaries and neighborhoods play out in the birth, decline, and redevelopment of Corktown.

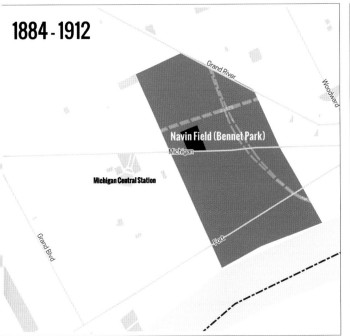

**1884 - 1912**

Grand River
Woodward
Navin Field (Bennet Park)
Michigan
Michigan Central Station
Grand Blvd
Fort

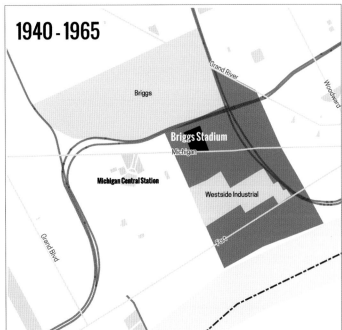

**1940 - 1965**

Grand River
Woodward
Briggs
Briggs Stadium
Michigan
Michigan Central Station
Westside Industrial
Grand Blvd
Fort

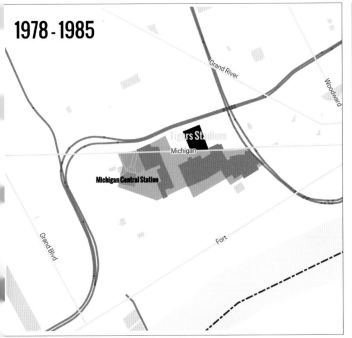

**1978 - 1985**

Grand River
Woodward
Tigers Stadium
Michigan
Michigan Central Station
Grand Blvd
Fort

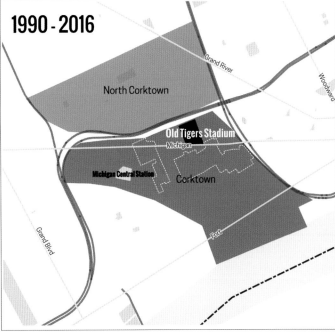

**1990 - 2016**

Grand River
Woodward
North Corktown
Old Tigers Stadium
Michigan
Michigan Central Station
Corktown
Grand Blvd
Fort

# CHANGES IN THE LAND: HAMTRAMCK

Named for Colonel Jean-François Hamtramck, who fought for the Americans in the Revolutionary War, the city of Hamtramck is an oddity, surrounded by the city of Detroit. The story of Hamtramck's evolution—or rather, its shrinking borders—is more so the story of Detroit's desire to annex land than Hamtramck's decline.

If you live anywhere on the east side or in the Grosse Pointes, you're more of a Hamtramckan than you might think.

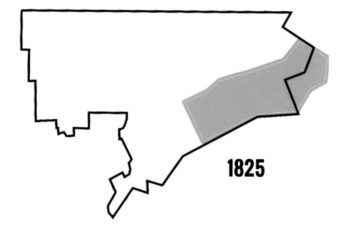

1825

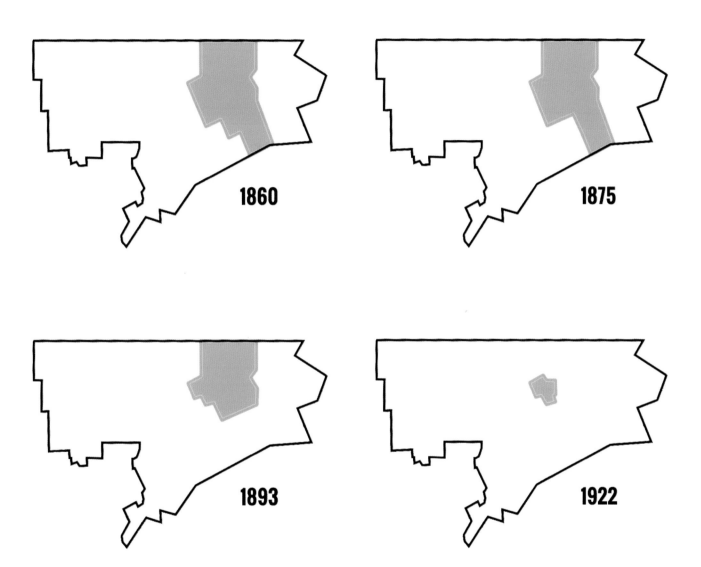

1860

1875

1893

1922

**Home Owners' Loan Corporation**
Grade "C"
Grade "D"

# THE LEGACY OF REDLINING

Like much of America, Detroit's history of racial discrimination is evident in its housing policies, which in turn contributed to job discrimination, interpersonal racism, and continued racial inequity of opportunity.

The Home Owners' Loan Corporation (1933–1939), which would become the Federal Housing Administration, graded neighborhoods or "redlined" them based on the race of people living there. The redlined grades were then used to deny financial services and home loans to Black Americans.

The redlined and yellow areas of Detroit were targeted for "urban renewal" in the 1960s, which displaced thousands of Black residents to public housing complexes.

Today, these areas of Detroit have more vacancy than others, either because the redlined properties were managed by slumlords whose properties deteriorated more quickly, or because renewal efforts didn't consider the displacement of Black residents.

# THE GREEN BOOK

*The Negro Motorist Green Book* was a directory of a different kind of "underground railroad" for the Jim Crow era, allowing Black Americans to map the most welcoming routes to reach vacation spots, hotels, beauty parlors, service stations, mechanic shops, and more. *The Green Book* regularly included state-specific traffic laws and issues for Black motorists to watch out for.

The 1937 edition was limited to New York City, but by 1938, it was "listing all of the States east of the Mississippi River." Detroit first appeared in the 1938 edition of *The Green Book* with listings for nine hotels, two night clubs, and one service station. They are located in a very small area where there was a high density of nonwhite residents.

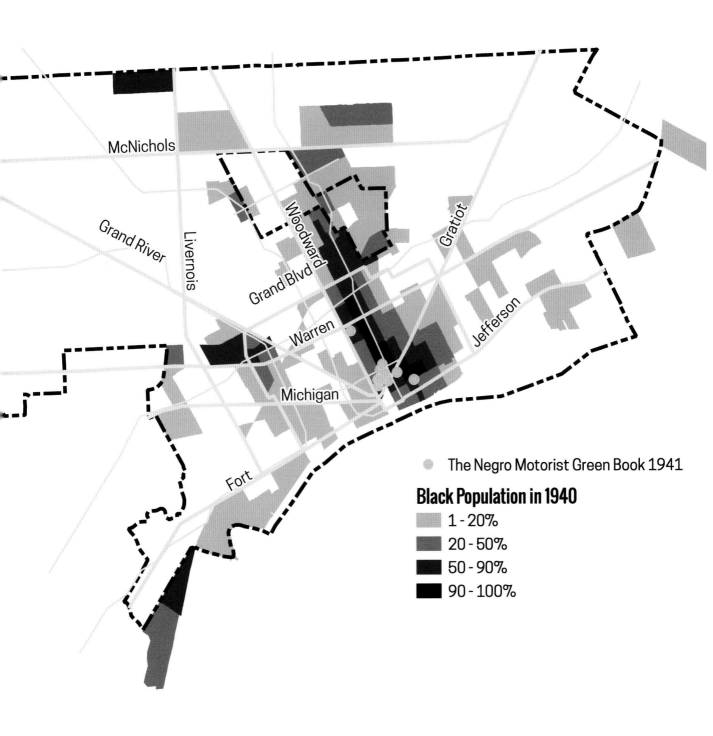

McNichols

Grand River

Livernois

Woodward

Grand Blvd

Gratiot

Warren

Jefferson

Michigan

Fort

The Negro Motorist Green Book 1941

**Black Population in 1940**

1 - 20%

20 - 50%

50 - 90%

90 - 100%

By 1949, Detroit's extensive listings demonstrate how it became a mecca for Black tourism and entertainment at the height of Paradise Valley. Not surprisingly, *The Green Book* locations match exactly with areas of Detroit with more Black residents (due to restrictive and discriminatory housing policies). The 1949 edition also included listings for Canada and Mexico.

By later editions, in 1963, a defining year for the Civil Rights Movement, *The Green Book* lacked welcoming amenity listings and instead included pages on national and local laws so that African American motorists could know their rights while traveling.

McNichols

Grand River

Livernois

Woodward

Gratiot

Grand Blvd

Warren

Jefferson

Michigan

Fort

The Negro Motorist Green Book 1949

**Black Population in 1940**

1 - 20%

20 - 50%

50 - 90%

90 - 100%

## GOOD NEIGHBORHOODS INITIATIVE, 2003
## SKILLMAN FOUNDATION

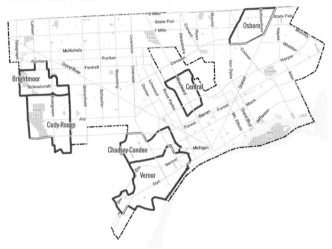

## MASTER PLANNING NEIGHBORHOODS, 2004

## PLANNING CLUSTERS, 2007

## CITY COUNCIL DISTRICTS, 2012

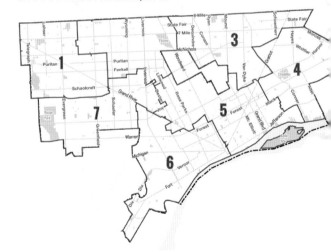

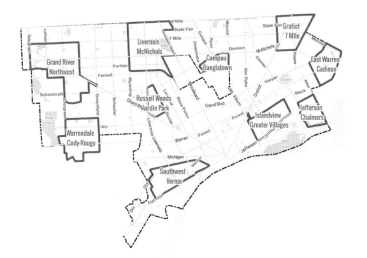

# GOVERNANCE AND NEIGHBORHOOD AREAS

The number of disparate boundaries in Detroit is both fascinating and befuddling: police scout car areas, curbside trash pickup zones, fire hydrant company areas, and on and on. All of these boundaries are actively used to plan the city's future.

**Good Neighborhoods Initiative, 2003:** The Skillman Foundation used census data to identify the top areas where the most children lived in the city. They spent ten years providing targeted investments in community organizations, schools, and place-making improvements.

**Planning Clusters, 2007:** The City Planning Commission decided to break the city up into ten clusters based on the Master Plan neighborhoods in order to focus development work. These clusters are still written into the official work of the Planning and Development Department.

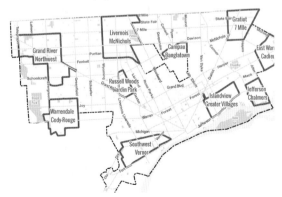

**Strategic Neighborhood Fund, 2016:** Mayor Duggan created a public-private fund to initiate "neighborhood" planning work in a few handpicked areas. The Strategic Neighborhood Fund areas do not align with any other "neighborhood" boundaries. Hundreds of millions have been raised to support development work in these areas.

**Master Plan Neighborhoods, 2004:** These boundaries are the legacy of the United Community Services/United Way Community Services "subcommunities" first developed in 1951 and drawn along census tract boundaries so that census data could be used to compare areas. These fifty-four areas have been the official "neighborhoods" since that time and remain so since the city's Master Plan has not been updated since 2004.

**City Council Districts, 2012:** The city voted to elect representatives by geographic district as part of the City Charter revision. The final boundaries only align with census block boundaries, making it difficult to match any demographic data to districts.

**Neighborhoods, 2016:** Mayor Duggan's new Department of Neighborhoods (DON) adopted an interesting and controversial set of some 200+ "neighborhood" boundaries largely based on the work of a local tech company and not based on community feedback.

Palmer

McNichols

Grand River

Livernois

Woodward

Chandler

Gratiot

Grand Blvd

Rouge
Park

Warren

Jefferson

Belle
Isle

Michigan

Fort

# INVESTMENT ZONES

Detroit's long-term decline has spurred spatial zones of care where nonprofits and foundations have focused their funding and technical support. Each decade seems to include a different set of focus regions within the city.

This map shows different overlapping investment zones over the last two decades in Detroit, from nonprofit efforts to mayoral initiatives.

The Skillman Foundation's Good Neighborhoods Initiative focused on areas where there were high numbers of children. Local Initiatives Support Corporation (LISC) works to support community resilience and economic opportunity. Many other organizations utilize these same areas, creating compounded benefits and impacts.

Federal programs have introduced Renaissance Zones, Renewal Community Zones, and Opportunity Zones to offer tax incentives and reduce tax burdens to spur growth.

Mayors often handpick neighborhoods for investment, such as Kwame Kilpatrick's "Next Detroit Neighborhood Initiative," Dennis Archer's "Community Reinvestment Strategy," and Mike Duggan's "Strategic Neighborhood Fund."

# MIDTOWN CREATION AND EXPANSION

Since 2000, the area known as Midtown has seen rapid expansion. Even though Midtown is largely a conglomeration of various institutional partners and acts as an economic driver, there is no official geographic demarcation, which has seemingly allowed Midtown to continue reaching northward. In many instances, the authority Midtown Detroit Inc. offers incentives in an area before officially annexing it for inclusion in its official brochures.

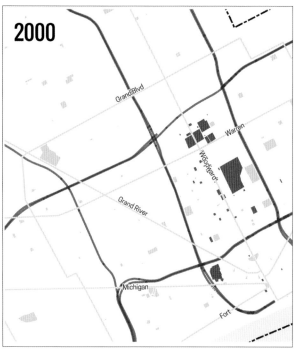

In early 2011, the University Cultural Center Association merged with the New Center Council and formally began doing work as Midtown Detroit, Inc. The organization has expanded its staff and geographic footprint, increased its real estate investment activities, and is implementing additional programs. This new footprint incorporates TechTown and the New Center area, which will allow the organization to work more closely with HFHS, University Preparatory Schools, the College for Creative Studies, and many other anchors.

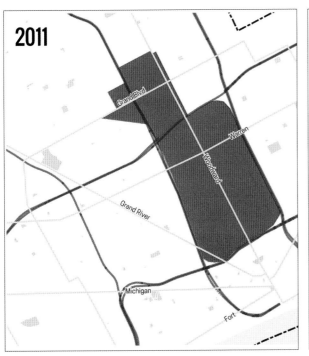
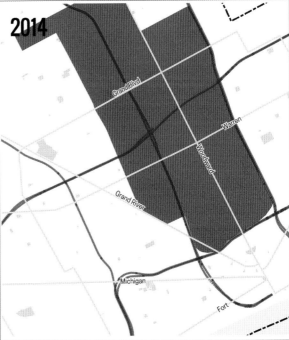

Forest

Canfield

Willis

Alexand...

Selden

2nd Ave

Brainard

# Cass Corridor
# Midtown

Martin Luther King

Grand River

# CASS CORRIDOR VS. MIDTOWN

Perhaps one of the starkest examples of the naming and claiming of space in Detroit is what is often found reported in the media. Although they are the same spatial zone, crimes are reported as happening in Cass Corridor, while new restaurant openings happen in Midtown.

The "Data, Mapping, and Research Justice" workshop participants at Allied Media Projects interviewed 30 people along Cass Avenue, Second Avenue, and Third Street. People that they met along these streets were asked simply, "What do you call this area?"

Sometimes the surveyors' data collection clipboards made people wary, but often the clipboards invited more questions, making it easy to engage people on the street, at restaurants, and waiting for the bus.

Midtown was the more commonly referenced place-name, but overall, the data gave a fairly even representation of the area. If anything, the responses collected from people shows the well-documented debate over the naming of neighborhoods and who has a right to name it.

One individual interviewed at MLK noted:

"They [white people] call it Midtown."

And what do you call it?

"Doesn't matter, they call it Midtown."

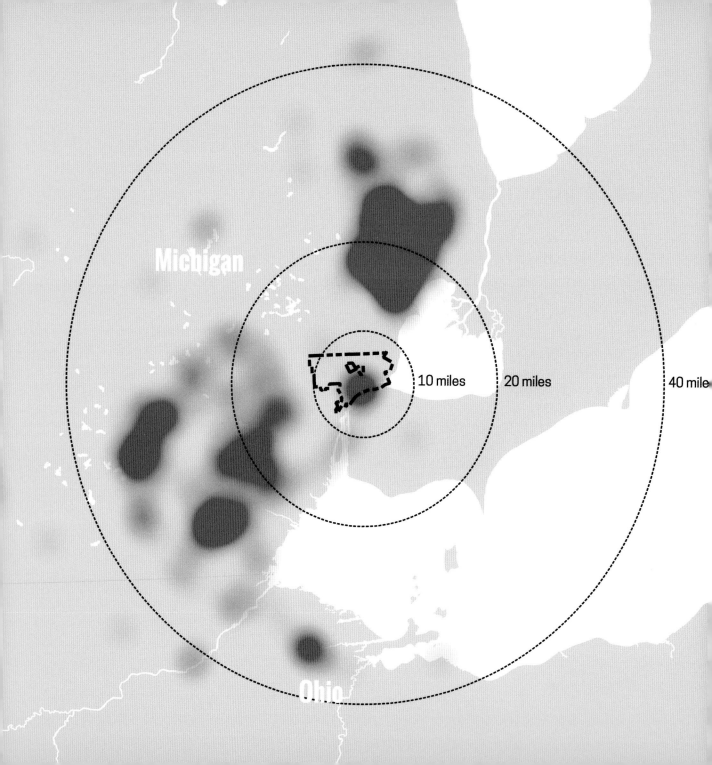

Michigan

10 miles    20 miles    40 mile

Ohio

# EASTERN MARKET REGIONAL FOODSHED

Detroit's Eastern Market is known as a regional food hub, where producers and consumers meet to connect the food system supply chain. Growers and farmers from the list of weekly Saturday market vendors were mapped to discover the system's extent.

While Eastern Market's reach extends across state and national borders into Ohio and Ontario, the vast majority of food hub participants are within forty miles of the market. There are a very small number of growers from within the city of Detroit, and the majority come from Macomb and St. Clair counties to the northeast. These areas are, not surprisingly, at the edge of the urban–rural transition.

Graffiti Tickets
- Not responsible By City Dismissal
- Responsible By Default
- Murals in the Market - Wall Locations

Woodward

Gratiot

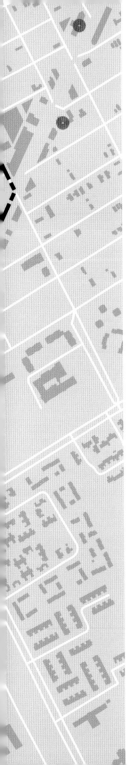

# EASTERN MARKET MURALS VS. GRAFFITI

Recently, the city has ramped up ticketing for blight violators—in particular, properties with graffiti. In some reported cases, the graffiti tickets included sanctioned murals and street art around Eastern Market. Such tickets led the mayor to apologize and dismiss all graffiti tickets for murals and signs, but the majority of businesses ticketed for graffiti along Division St. and Winder St. remain responsible for paying their fees.

Legend:

- ■ Art Houses
- ● Clocks
- ● Dots
- ● Numbers
- ● Taxis
- ▭ Heidelberg Project Boundary

Warren

Gratiot

Woodward

# HEIDELBERG ART ARTIFACTS

Tyree Guyton's Heidelberg Project has defined the near east side of Detroit for more than thirty years. The McDougall-Hunt area is typically where people visit the Heidelberg Project houses and works of art, but Tyree has spread his influence from Mt. Elliott to Eastern Market.

From March 2017 to May 2018, I began driving the streets one-by-one beyond the Heidelberg Street core. Tyree has a very recognizable painted dot, often paints a "1-2-3" number series and clocks, clocks, clocks.

At the end of May 2018, I noticed the graffiti and demolition crews were starting to remove many of the artifacts that I found. The bones of an old brick house were demolished and a Tyree clock artifact was lost. The graffiti team did a sweep of Mt. Elliott, and numerous clocks and dots were covered in a layer of brown paint. As a result, many of these mapped artifacts no longer exist.

The Polka Dot House is the iconic symbol of the Heidelberg Project, but Tyree painted dots across the Eastside and likely painted more clocks on vacant, abandoned, and blighted structures in the neighborhood.

Grand Blvd

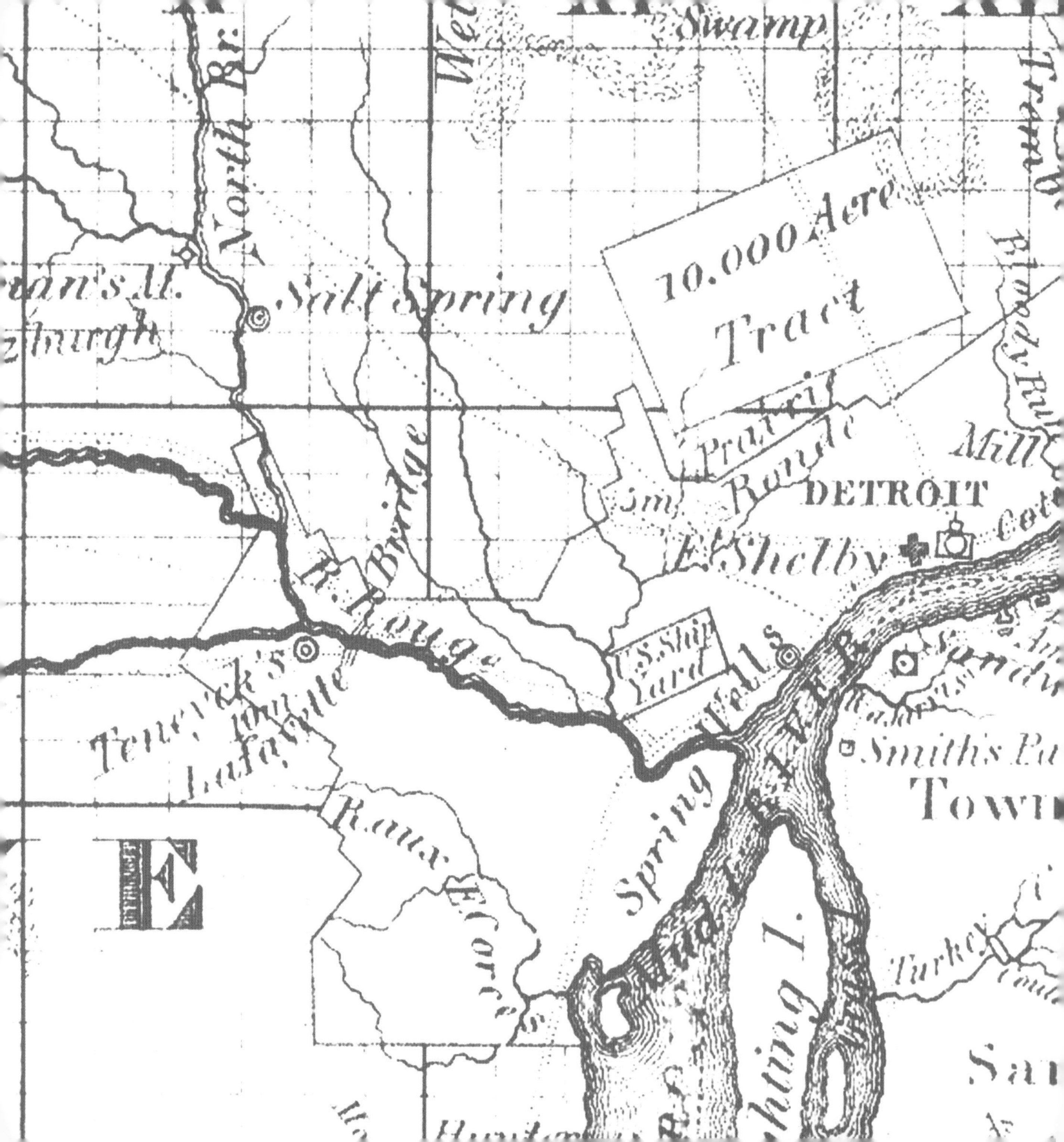

North Br.

West

Swamp

Tram'

Bloody

ran's M.
zhurgh

Salt Spring

10,000 Acre
Tract

Prairie
Ronde

Mill

DETROIT

5m

E. Shelby

Cott

R. Bridge

R. Rouge

U.S. Ship
Yard

Spring Wells

HURON R.

Sandw

Teneeck's
Lafayette

Smith's Pa

E

Raux

Eau

Town

Spring

Grosse I.

Turke

ighting I.

Sa

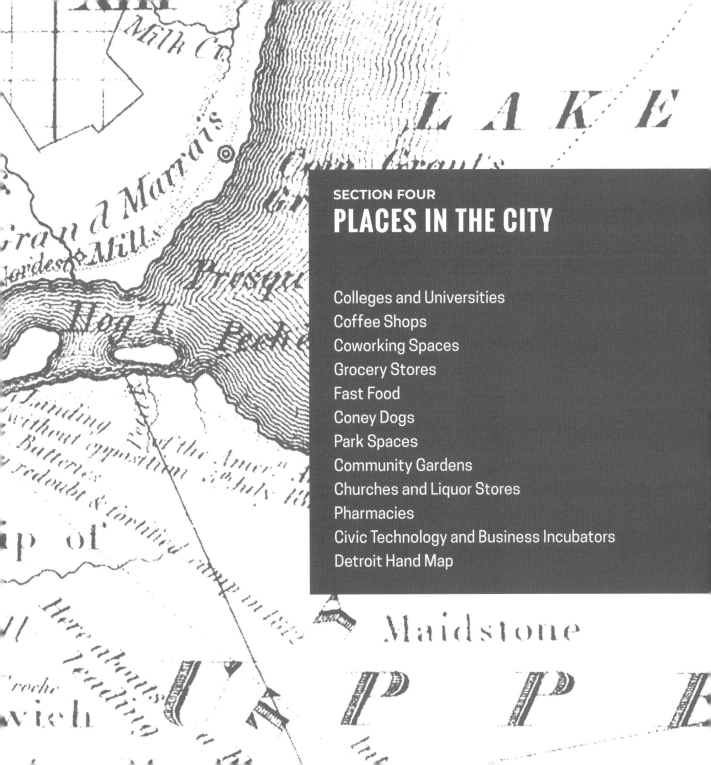

SECTION FOUR
# PLACES IN THE CITY

Colleges and Universities
Coffee Shops
Coworking Spaces
Grocery Stores
Fast Food
Coney Dogs
Park Spaces
Community Gardens
Churches and Liquor Stores
Pharmacies
Civic Technology and Business Incubators
Detroit Hand Map

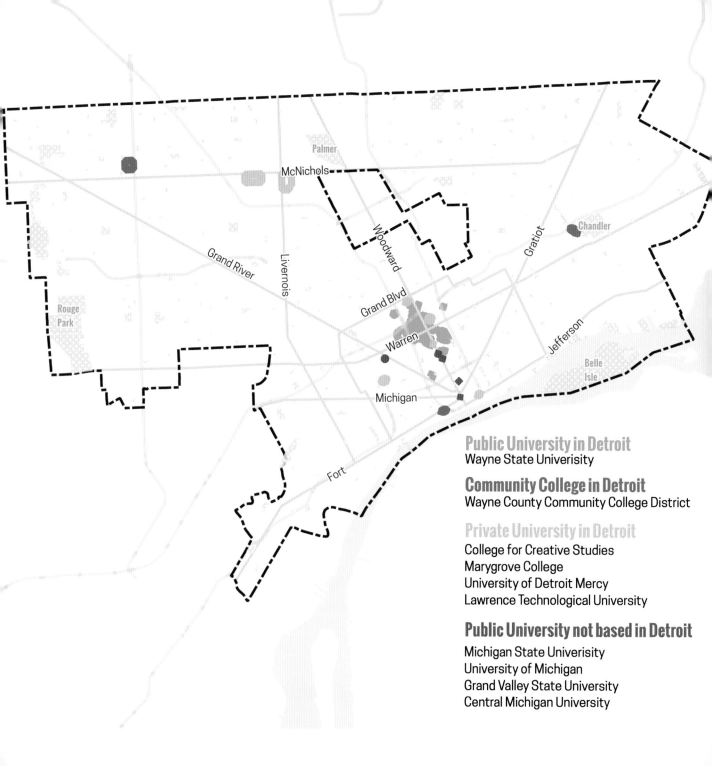

**Public University in Detroit**
Wayne State Univerisity

**Community College in Detroit**
Wayne County Community College District

**Private University in Detroit**
College for Creative Studies
Marygrove College
University of Detroit Mercy
Lawrence Technological University

**Public University not based in Detroit**
Michigan State Univerisity
University of Michigan
Grand Valley State University
Central Michigan University

# COLLEGES AND UNIVERSITIES

Detroit has been host to a number of colleges and universities from its founding. As Michigan's largest city and former state capital, Detroit held the greatest number of highly educated individuals in the state.

In 1817, Justice Woodward wrote up plans for the "University of Michigania," with 13 departments. The building was constructed at Bates and Congress, but due to disagreements over educational ideas, controversies over the land, and general mismanagement, the university never really took off. Land that had been previously earmarked for a new Michigan state capital soon became the new University of Michigan in Ann Arbor under the leadership of Henry Tappan in 1837.

In recent years, Detroit has seen an influx of college and university satellite sites. The University of Michigan (UM) Detroit Center opened in 2005, and Michigan State University (MSU) Detroit Center opened in 2009.

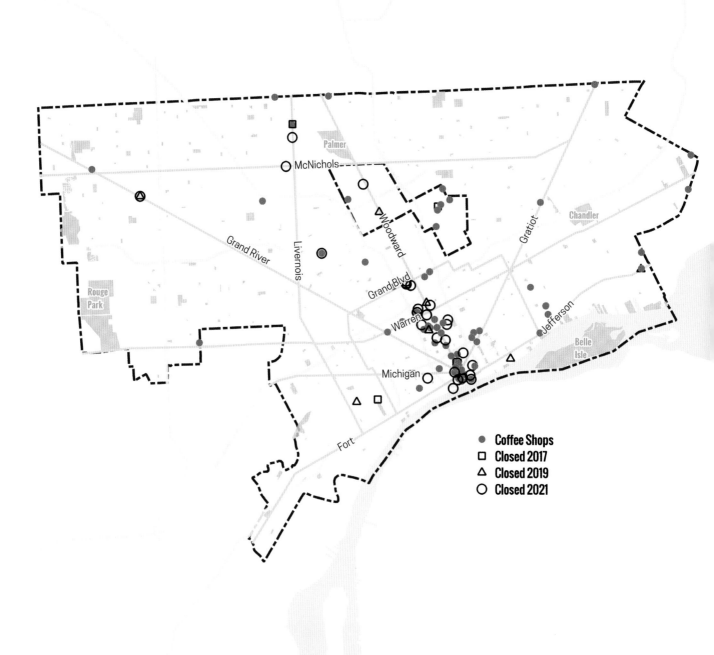

Palmer

McNichols

Woodward

Chandler

Grand River

Livernois

Gratiot

Rouge
Park

Grand Blvd

Warren

Jefferson

Belle
Isle

Michigan

Fort

● **Coffee Shops**
□ **Closed 2017**
△ **Closed 2019**
○ **Closed 2021**

# COFFEE SHOPS

In 2015, the chief executive and chief economist of Zillow wrote that Starbucks fuels gentrification and higher housing prices. The problem is that Starbucks stores often locate in wealthier neighborhoods, so it becomes difficult to say what is the true relational direction. There are very few Starbucks locations in Detroit.

Community groups often request coffee shops as community gathering spaces. The majority of coffee shops in Detroit are independent and community focused. Neighborhoods adjacent to the 7.2-square-mile Downtown-Midtown investment zone are seeing expansion, and new coffee shops are opening up, adding to the existing density of coffee options.

Palmer

McNichols

Woodward

Gratiot

Chandler

Grand River

Livernois

Rouge
Park

Grand Blvd

Jefferson

Warren

Belle
Isle

Michigan

Fort

● Coworking Spaces
□ Closed 2017
△ Closed 2019
○ Closed 2021

# COWORKING SPACES

An important piece of growing Detroit's technology allure has been the ability to find and collaborate with like-minded people. Coworking spaces have found a booming market to offer space and opportunities to collaborate. However, coworking remains an exclusive opportunity based on monthly pricing plans.

Coworking remains a predominantly Downtown and Midtown activity with a few neighborhood-based opportunities outside of the 7.2-square-mile area of concentrated revitalization.

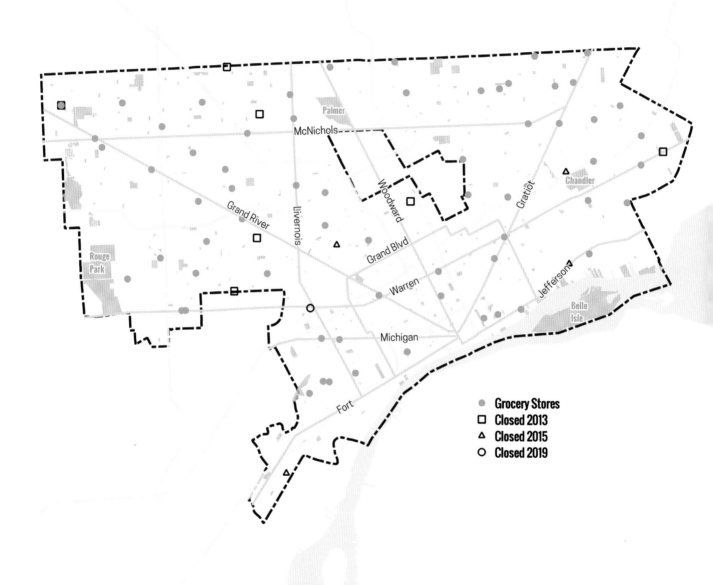

Palmer

McNichols

Woodward

Chandler

Gratiot

Grand River

Livernois

Rouge
Park

Grand Blvd

Jefferson

Belle
Isle

Warren

Michigan

Fort

**Grocery Stores**
□ Closed 2013
△ Closed 2015
○ Closed 2019

# GROCERY STORES

Detroit has always had independent grocery stores, but today they make up the majority of available grocer options rather than being one choice among many. There are only four national chain supermarkets in the city limits.

The grocery store landscape changes regularly in Detroit. There have been a handful of openings and closings every year, but the trend is that Detroit loses grocery stores every year. Some get bought up by dollar stores, others burn down, and still more simply become vacant as the cost of doing business is too great.

Fast Food
Pizza
Coney Island

# FAST FOOD

Detroit is better understood as a "food swamp" rather than a "food desert." There are food options all over the city, and most are more conveniently located than a grocery store.

Fast food is Detroit's second-largest food industry behind the snack foods and beverages group. Detroit has many major chain fast food restaurants, but also a handful of local chains, like Captain Jay's Fish and Chicken.

Detroit fast food is particularly interesting for its plethora of pizza takeout options as well as the regional favorite, Coney Island restaurants.

Detroit-style pizza has gained national recognition recently both by Pizza Hut (which has no locations in Detroit) and *Food & Wine* magazine. Buddy's Pizza claims the origin story of Detroit-style pizza. The blue square pan used to bake the pizza came from an automotive factory, where it had previously been used to hold nuts and bolts for cars.

# CONEY DOGS

The coney dog was born in Detroit. The 2012 book titled *Coney Detroit* attributes the "coney dog" to Greek immigrants who likely passed through Ellis Island in New York (near the birthplace of the hot dog, Coney Island).

Coney dogs were cheap and quick, allowing them to propagate outside of Detroit's major factories. Workers had short lunches and limited budgets—the coney dog was the answer.

Today, there are multiple opportunities to eat at a Coney Island restaurant or diner. There are a few coney chains in the southeast Michigan region, and in the city of Detroit there are some coney clusters. Detroit's Downtown is home to the Lafayette versus American rivalry, Northwest has Coney Islands right next to each other and includes Nicky D's, while east of the State Fairgrounds sports a string of coneys mostly along Conant Street.

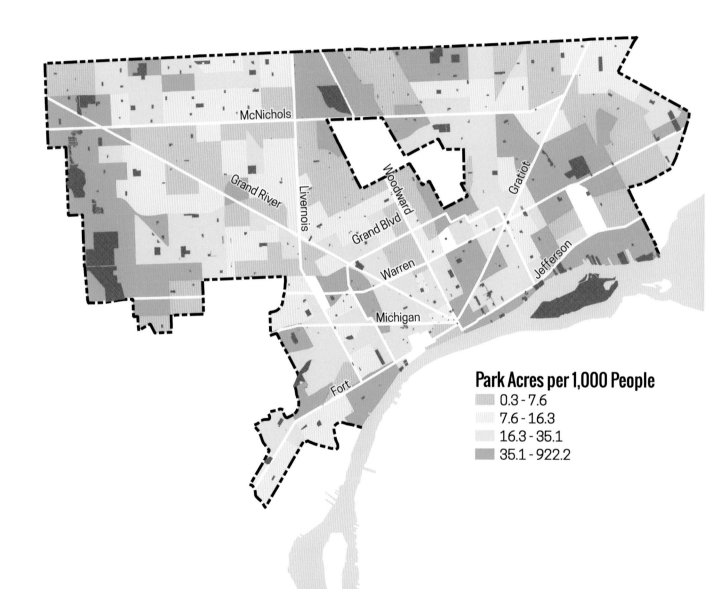

McNichols

Grand River

Livernois

Woodward

Grand Blvd

Gratiot

Warren

Jefferson

Michigan

Fort

**Park Acres per 1,000 People**

0.3 - 7.6
7.6 - 16.3
16.3 - 35.1
35.1 - 922.2

# PARK SPACES

There has been a lot of change to Detroit's parks over the years, including the near closing of over fifty of them during Mayor Bing's time, an influx of funding to keep them open, the widespread adoption of parks by community groups, a new parks master plan, and the dedication of $11.7 million to help forty smaller neighborhood parks in the summer of 2021.

Some of Detroit's more populated areas have much smaller parks. With more people and smaller park spaces, that leaves fewer acres per person. Residents of the city benefit from Detroit's many large parks; however, the key missing variable here is safety and crime in the parks as well as community perceptions of using park space for leisure or physical activity.

Palmer

McNichols

Woodward

Chandler

Grand River

Livernois

Gratiot

Grand Blvd

Rouge
Park

Warren

Jefferson

Belle
Isle

Michigan

Fort

# COMMUNITY GARDENS

Detroit is a global leader in urban agriculture, showing the world how to utilize space and bring people together around growing food. Mayor Pingree first allowed residents to farm vacant land in 1893, and the recent citywide Farm-a-Lot program under Mayor Coleman Young has been a great success.

This is a map of all the past and present community gardens hosted by community groups, churches, and nonprofits, as well as large-scale urban farming over an acre in size.

There is a great amount of opportunity in Detroit for urban growing, but it is not without its challenges. A number of large-scale operations have reported multiple break-ins and theft of equipment.

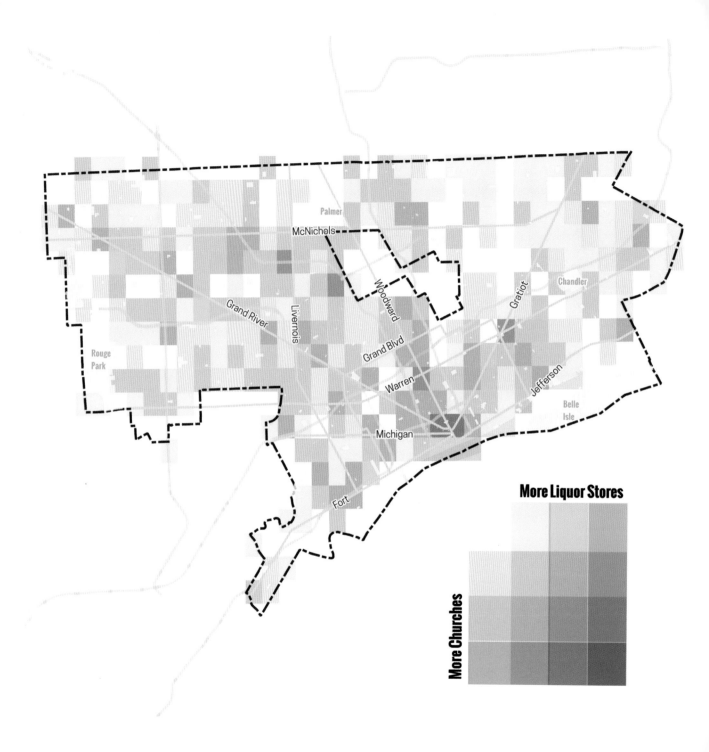

**More Liquor Stores**

**More Churches**

# CHURCHES AND LIQUOR STORES

Driving along Van Dyke, where you can see church after church (many abandoned) interspersed with liquor stores, gave me the idea of examining which type of location dominated Detroit's landscape.

Churches in Detroit come in all shapes and sizes, from megachurches that cover an entire block to converted storefront churches to the smattering of beautiful historic churches large and small.

There is a strong concentration of liquor licenses in Downtown, which isn't surprising with the density of restaurants and bars. However, there are other notable areas with a high number of liquor licenses that dot the city.

Palmer

McNichols

Woodward

Chandler

Gratiot

Grand River

Livernois

Rouge
Park

Grand Blvd.

Jefferson

Warren

Belle
Isle

Michigan

Fort

# PHARMACIES

In the March 2017 report, "Going the Distance: Big Data on Resident Access to Everyday Goods," the J. P. Morgan Chase Institute identified pharmacies as a leading accessibility point for Detroit residents. The report compared data for both New York City and Detroit and found that in both cities, the majority of residents shopped for retail goods outside of their twenty-minute neighborhood area.

Pharmacies, which were 0.9 miles away on average, were ranked first, while grocery stores, which were 1.4 miles away on average, came in second. The analysis was run with ZIP codes filling in for neighborhoods and with ZIP code centroids being used to calculate distance, which causes some issues when trying to measure the distance between residents to retailers.

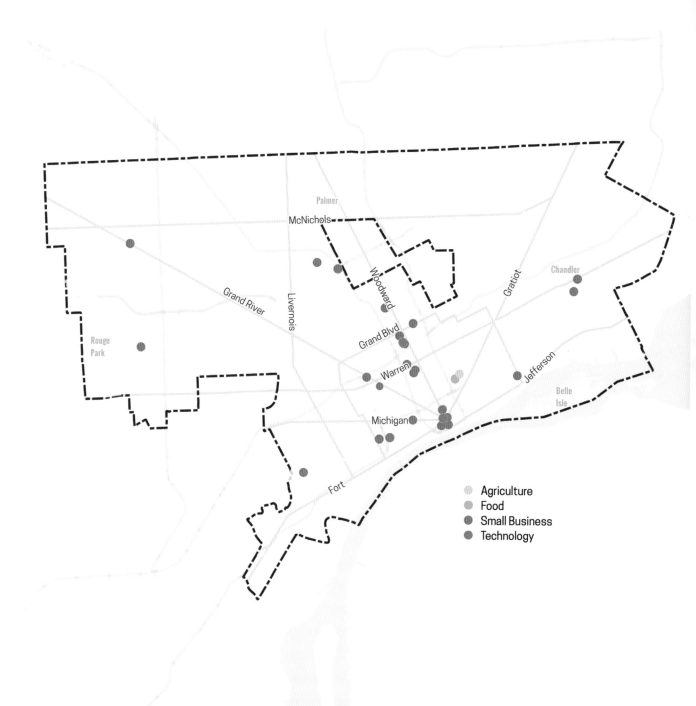

Palmer

McNichols

Woodward

Chandler

Grand River

Livernois

Gratiot

Rouge
Park

Grand Blvd

Jefferson

Warren

Belle
Isle

Michigan

Fort

Agriculture
Food
Small Business
Technology

# CIVIC TECHNOLOGY AND BUSINESS INCUBATORS

Innovation is a staple in Detroit. The introduction of new technologies was welcomed by local government in an effort to improve communication and streamline services.

The city has numerous technology hubs, makerspaces, and centers of innovation in business, health, food, and more.

If you are interested in launching a business in Detroit, there are multiple training programs, fellowships, and funding competitions to help get your idea off the ground.

If you want to start a food business, Food-Lab and 25 other resources can help. If you hope to launch a technology company, Techtown and many of its member groups have the tools to share. If you want to become a successful urban farmer, there's even the Urban Roots training program, since most traditional business incubators don't understand vegetables and crop rotation.

Detroit's robust ecosystem of training, support, and opportunity has been fostered from the grassroots and support by large corporations, like the new Apple Developer Training Academy launched in 2020.

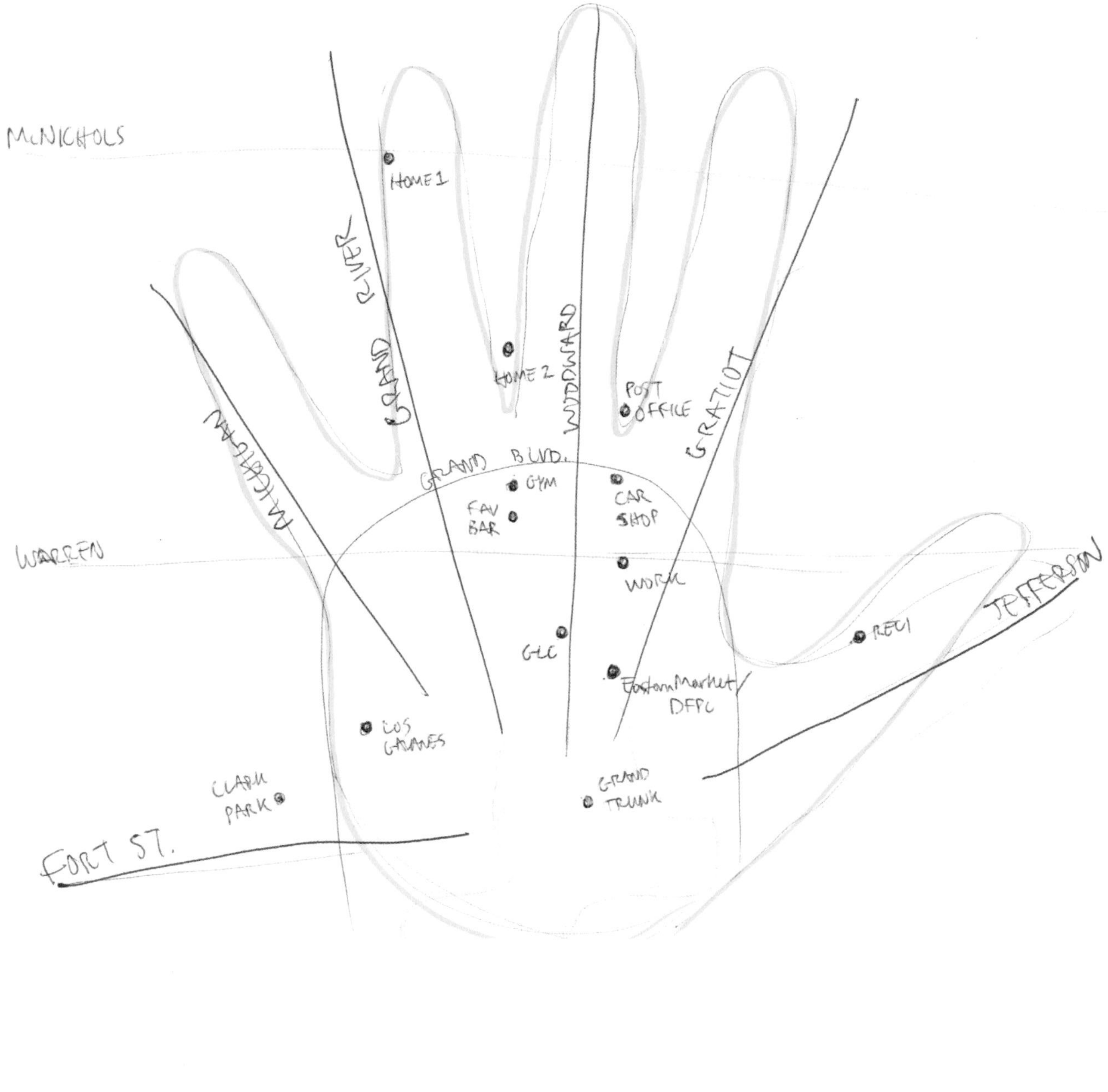

MCNICHOLS

GRAND RIVER

WOODWARD

GRATIOT

MICHIGAN

HOME 1

HOME 2

POST OFFICE

GRAND BLVD.

GYM

FAV BAR

CAR SHOP

WARREN

WORK

JEFFERSON

GLC

REC

Eastern Market / DFC

LOS GALANES

GRAND TRUNK

CLARK PARK

FORT ST.

# DETROIT HAND MAP

If you are a Michigander, then you've most likely used your hand as a map of the state's lower peninsula throughout your life. You can also do the same if you are a Detroiter.

The hand map of Detroit was first introduced in the late 1960s. It was documented in the Detroit Geographic Expedition and Institute's Field Notes I publication. It was meant to help members of the group and student researchers so they wouldn't get lost on "expeditions" around the city. The source of the hand map example is supposedly a Check Cab driver.

This is an amended version of the original hand map. The spread-out fingers become the spoke streets or historic trails leading to downtown Detroit. Grand Boulevard follows the palm of the hand. This example adds a sixth finger to include Southwest Detroit's Ford Street.

Since 2013, DETROITography has collected over 300 hand maps from residents, students, and visitors. These collected memory maps present an alternative set of data and memories about the city.

Submit yours at: submit.detroitography.com/submit

# SOURCES

**p. 2**: 1904 Sanborn map of the Central Business District of Detroit

**p. 6**: From *Histoire générale des Voyages* (Paris, 1746-1759; 15 volumes) by l'Abbé Antoine François Prévost with maps and views by Jacques-Nicolas Bellin; made available online by Columbia University

**p. 10**: DETROITography.com

**p. 12**: 1835 map of the city of Detroit in the state of Michigan by John Farmer. Library of Congress.

**p. 14**: 1889 bird's eye view—showing about three miles square—of the central portion of the city of Detroit, Michigan. Calvert Lithographing Co. Library of Congress.

**p. 15**: Hand drawn map of Detroit with major roadways by the author.

**p. 16-17**: Digital map of Detroit with major roadways labeled by the author. Data came from the Detroit Open Data Portal and SEMCOG Open Data Portal.

**p. 22**: Digitized map of so-called Indian trails georeferenced from the 1931 Archaeological Atlas of Michigan by Wilbert B. Hinsdale. University of Michigan Digital General Collection.

**p. 23**: 1820 map of the Detroit River survey. A collection of maps, charts, drawings, surveys, etc., published from time to time, by order of the two houses of Congress. Library of Congress.

**p. 24**: 1826 map of the surveyed part of the territory of Michigan on a scale of 8 miles per inch. John Farmer and V. Balch and S. Stiles. Library of Congress.

**p. 25-29**: City of Detroit road layer from the Detroit Open Data Portal. DETROITography, 2013.

**p. 30**: The overlaid results of first 100 images that appeared in a Google image search for "map of Detroit" on 11/24/2013. DETROITography, 2013.

**p. 32**: Municipal borders from SEMCOG Open Data Portal. DETROITography, 2013.

**p. 34-35**: Media mentions sourced from Aaron Foley's 2012 article "Where exactly is the heart of Detroit?" (Mlive) as well as a Google search for other media mentions for "heart of Detroit." DETROITography, 2017.

**p. 36–37**: Municipal borders from SEMCOG Open Data Portal.

**p. 39**: City boundary comparisons digitized from Google Maps using WGS84 web Mercator projection. DETROI-Tography, 2015.

**p. 40**: Annexation boundaries digitized from the "Manual, County of Wayne, Michigan 1926."

**p. 41**: Color fold out map of "City of Detroit indicating growth by Annexation 1806 to 1926" scanned from "Manual, County of Wayne, Michigan 1926."

**p. 42**: City Council Districts and ZIP codes datasets from Detroit Open Data Portal.

**p. 43**: Pheasant sightings in Detroit compiled from WDET's public map of listener submissions along with other relevant pheasant sightings mentioned on Detroit social media and message boards, such as DetroitYes!. DETROITography, 2016.

**p. 45**: Dog name data shared by Canine to Five, a dog boarding and grooming company in Detroit and Ferndale.

**p. 51**: Data from the US Census via the CDC Social Vulnerability Index, 2018.

**p. 52**: Data from Detroit Open Data Portal. Greenways, 2016.

**p. 53**: Data from Detroit Open Data Portal. Bus alighting, 2017.

**p. 54**: Data from Detroit Open Data Portal. Parcel Points, 2020.

**p. 56**: Data from Detroit Open Data Portal. Parcel Map, 2020.

**p. 58**: Foreclosure data (2009–2013) from Data Driven Detroit's data portal. Eviction data (2009–2013) shared via Detroit News FOIA request to 36th District Court.

**p. 60**: Map of the city of Detroit, Michigan, 1904, showing wards and election districts. Published in Detroit by Calvert Lithographing Co. MSU Libraries Digital Collection, Map Library.

**p. 61**: Precinct-level election data shared by Bridge Michigan.

**p. 62–65**: US census population estimates for race and ethnicity from American Community Survey 2019, five year estimates. One dot represents 50 people.

**p. 66**: US census population estimates from American Community Survey 2019, five year estimates.

**p. 68**: Data on life expectancy (2004–2013) in Wayne County ZIP codes courtesy of the VCU Center on Society and Health. DETROITography, 2017.

**p. 69**: Data on medically underserved areas and populations from the Health Resources and Services Administration (HRSA). DETROITography, 2017.

**p. 71-73**: Chronic disease small area estimates generated by the CDC 500 Cities project.

**p. 74**: COVID-19 case data from the Detroit Health Department tracking dashboard.

**p. 76**: Data on "Arsenal of Democracy" factory locations from the Detroit Historical Society. Data on "Arsenal of Health" participating locations collected by the author via news reports. DETROITography, 2020.

**p. 81**: User submitted "neighborhood" areas collected (2013) in Site Control and shared by Loveland Technologies. DETROITography, 2016.

**p. 83**: Neighborhood areas drawn by the author based on Silas Farmer's writing in "The History of Detroit and Michigan," 1884. DETROITography, 2014.

**p. 85**: Data on Corktown boundaries and naming sourced from "The History of Detroit and Michigan" (1884), Urban Renewal project documents (1950), *Detroit Free Press* reports (1985), and the author's more recent engagements in Corktown (2011–2016). DETROITography, 2014.

**p. 86–87**: Boundaries of Hamtramck sourced from historical maps of Wayne County (1825, 1855, 1875, 1893, 1922). DETROITography, 2017.

**p. 88**: Dataset of Home Owners' Loan Corporation neighborhood grades downloaded from the University of Richmond's Digital Scholarship Lab project titled "Mapping Inequality."

**p. 90–93**: Data on *Green Book* locations collected by the author from the collection at NYPL's Schomburg Center for Research in Black Culture. DETROITography, 2018.

**p. 94–98**: Data from Data Driven Detroit's open data portal and the Detroit Open Data Portal.

**p. 100–101**: Data collected from various maps published by Midtown Detroit Inc. including from their "Stay Midtown" housing incentive program. DETROITography, 2015.

**p. 102**: Data collected by members of the 2015 "Data, Mapping, and Research Justice" workshop at Allied Media Projects. DETROITography, 2015.

**p. 104**: Data collected by the author from the vendor maps published by the Eastern Market Corporation. Vendor business addresses were then looked up and geocoded. DETROITography, 2018.

**p. 106–107**: Graffiti ticket data from the Detroit Open Data Portal. Wall locations collected by the author from the Murals in the Market webpage. DETROITography, 2016.

**p. 108–109**: Art artifact locations collected by the author while driving through the neighborhoods of Detroit's east side. DETROITography, 2018.

**p. 112**: Data collected by the author via Google search for university locations in Detroit as well as searching property ownership from the Detroit Open Data Portal, Parcel Map, 2020. DETROITography, 2014.

**p. 114**: Data collected and maintained by the author (2015–2021) via Google search and Google Places API. DETROITography, 2015, 2017, 2019, 2021.

**p. 116**: Data collected and maintained by the author (2014–2021) via Google search and Google Places API. DETROITography, 2014, 2017, 2019, 2021.

**p. 118**: Data collected and maintained by the author (Detroit Food Map initiative 2011–2021) via Google search, Google Street View, and in-person survey.

**p. 120**: Data from the Detroit Health Department Food Safety team.

**p. 122**: Data from the Detroit Health Department Food Safety team. DETROITography, 2017.

**p. 124**: Data from the Detroit Open Data Portal, Parks. Analysis conducted by the author applying a quarter mile buffer around each census tract and summing the park acres within each buffer zone. DETROITography, 2016.

**p. 126**: Community garden data from the Keep Growing Detroit Annual Report, 2019.

**p. 128**: Data from Data Driven Detroit's open data portal and the Michigan Liquor Control Commission. DETROITography, 2015.

**p. 130**: Data from the United Healthcare list of pharmacies in Detroit, 2016. DETROITography, 2017.

**p. 132**: Data collected by the author via Google search.

**p. 132**: The original published Detroit hand map came from the Detroit Geographical Expedition and Institute's "Field Notes I" in 1969. The original hand map was adapted and updated by the author. DETROITography, 2013.

# ABOUT THE AUTHOR

Alex B. Hill is GIS Director at Wayne State University and Project Director of the Detroit Food Map Initiative, which has been mapping nutritional access of Detroit grocery stores, corner stores, and farmers markets since 2011. He started the website DETROITography (detroitography.com) in an attempt to bring together various Detroit cartographers and their great work.

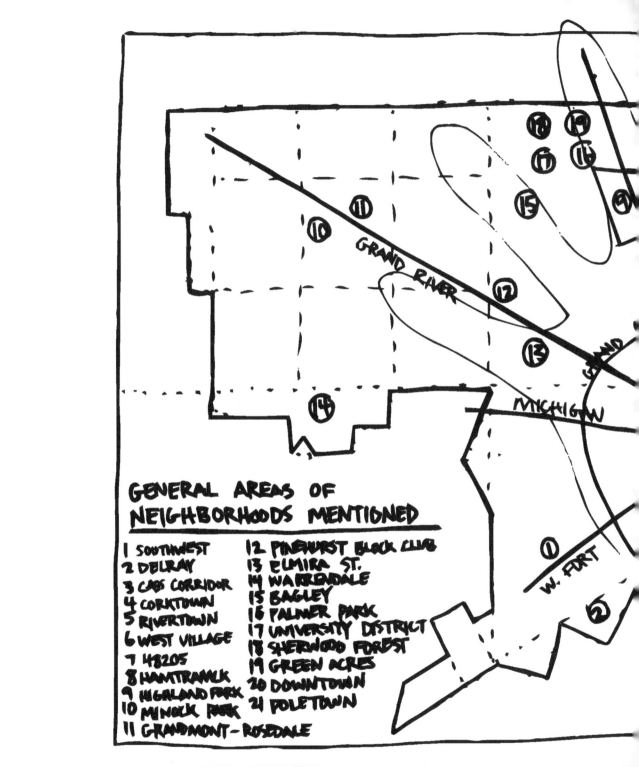

GENERAL AREAS OF
NEIGHBORHOODS MENTIONED

1 SOUTHWEST
2 DELRAY
3 CASS CORRIDOR
4 CORKTOWN
5 RIVERTOWN
6 WEST VILLAGE
7 48205
8 HAMTRAMCK
9 HIGHLAND PARK
10 MINOCK PARK
11 GRANDMONT-ROSEDALE

12 PINEHURST BLOCK CLUB
13 ELMIRA ST.
14 WARRENDALE
15 BAGLEY
16 PALMER PARK
17 UNIVERSITY DISTRICT
18 SHERWOOD FOREST
19 GREEN ACRES
20 DOWNTOWN
21 POLETOWN

GRAND RIVER

GRAND

MICHIGAN

W. FORT